THE OFFERING OF MAN

THE OFFERING

OF MAN

By

Harry Blamires

Introduction by

Bernard C. Newman

MOREHOUSE-BARLOW CO.

NEW YORK

1960

Manufactured in the United States of America

© HARRY BLAMIRES 1960

Library of Congress Catalogue Card No. 60-9769

CONTENTS

INTRODUCTION

THE theme of this book makes clear that the world
we are really interested in is the world we have put
our effort into for many years, the world of getting and having. We believe we can go on extend-
ing our holdings and our control. This world that
we have made and live in, without any practical
awareness of God, fills our minds. Mr. Blamires
shows that in a deeper sense the world we have constructed without God and His presence and action
among us, is necessarily a world dominated by self-
will and self-expression. Because God is kept outside the purpose and experience of every day, we are
not able to see the cause of our bitter frustrations.
To maintain ourselves, we have to go on acquiring
what things and what glory we can, and all the
while futility haunts us.

One great value of this book is that the Gospel
of Christ is seen once again to be so relevant to
man's persistent quandary. Without God our arms
are filled with the good things of creation and we
hold them to us even though our hearts are

wretched.   But God has come as Man into his own world, penetrating the whole of what man should do with his life and the good things of creation. In Christ's life and ministry and passion we see the need of our conversion.   We see how life is transfigured in the service of God, and, in the Cross, what evil we do in drawing everything into the service of our wills.   Evil is the perversion of the real nature of anything, the quality that makes it what it is.   If the divine order of God's creation is upset, God's authority and power no longer operate and man is corrupted.   It becomes necessary to restore man and help him direct his energies into the service of God.

Explicitly, the meaning of our Lord's life is shown in God offering Himself to us; and the meaning of our life is found in offering ourselves to Him.   The rule of the Christian life is discovered in the Incarnation: God offered Himself to us for our sake.   This world and all creatures in it are good.   God comes to re-fashion what is corrupt, to make man what he was intended to be.   This he cannot do himself without God working in him to draw him away from self-regard by His love. So the rule of the Incarnation, when it is followed, becomes in us the power of the Incarnation—the enabling love and strength to offer ourselves to

God, as God continually offers Himself to us.

Another insight given to us here is a conviction of our powerlessness in Christian living, because of our self-regard. Our lives and our world are not offered to God that His will may be fully done in them. In His Nativity our Lord did swiftly and surely what we slowly, painfully endeavor in the Christian life. The season of Advent is needed to prepare ourselves to respond to His self-offering because the stronghold of our pride and self-gratification never surrenders easily, and is frequently rearmed. Preparation for the Incarnation is needed if we are to be changed into temples for God the Holy Ghost. Preparation for the Passion and Resurrection is needed if the purpose and destiny of human life, through defeat and suffering, are to be shown in us. Only the power of God known through His self-offering on Christmas and on Good Friday working in us can make our offering to Him possible.

Finally, the repeated warnings in this book against partial offerings and compromises are exceedingly helpful. It is possible to cultivate a moral or emotional or physical type of religious life which is our own achievement; but the rule of the Incarnation cannot be compromised, it can only be broken. Our religious life must involve the offering to God of our full humanity, of all our faculties. Our Lord, by His Incarnation and His Crucifixion, leads us on to do as He has done—to make a genuine offering of ourselves in love to God and our fellow-creatures.

This will mean that we shall try and see ourselves as He does, without self-deception, without fear or blame for ourselves, and offer ourselves as we are. We then gladly give over to God all concern about results and moral improvement. These are His province and ours is obedience to Him. The power of the Incarnation is His coming to us as we are, to visit the full range of human life and enable the offering up to Him of all human desire and attachment and effort for His glory.

God's glory is our concern. Man's fulfillment is His purpose and His gift. It is "by His spirit that dwelleth in us," that we offer ourselves to Him.

BERNARD C. NEWMAN

Trinity Church
New York
November 1959

THE OFFERING OF MAN

1

OUR LORD'S HUMANITY

I SUSPECT that when a priest is in the pulpit, speaking of God's mysterious love or mercy, he will sometimes experience a sudden inward check and challenge. The fluent phrases, shaped in reflection, trimmed in delivery, are halted. The people before him are temporarily forgotten. There may be a sense of momentary exposure to the immensity of the divine, and a voice may ask, "How could you dare to speak of God?"

Certainly anyone who proposes to address his readers on the subject of God—His person, and His purpose for men—must necessarily experience, right at the start, a check of this kind. He can scarcely put pen to paper—jot down a few notes, a few headings and leading phrases—without feeling the momentary brake on the fingers and hearing the quiet challenge, "How dare you speak of God?"

How *can* we dare? How can *we* dare, when there are monks and nuns, vowed and withdrawn, living in hourly prayer and obedience, locked in the grip of the divine companionship, who yet say nothing? How can we dare when they, the wholly dedicated, the totally given, men and women dead to the world and alive only to God's love, are yet content to hold their peace? How can we dare when those who are most truly acquainted with God's person are readier to fold their hands again in prayer than to turn out new phrases to advertise Him? How can the mere writer have the effrontery to chatter about God?

These questions are not asked because they are rhetorically unanswerable: on the contrary, they are firmly and exactly answerable. We can speak about God, we can bandy His name between us, we can spin the facile sentences on paper which crudely hint at what He is and what He does— we can do all this, and do it legitimately, for a very good reason: because He is that kind of God. He is a God who has put Himself among men to be known and talked about and handled; to be looked at, pointed to, and described. Of course this is not the only, nor indeed the chief, truth about Him: He is also a God to be trembled at and grovelled before; a God of mystery and majesty before whom all heads are lowered, all eyes closed, and all tongues stilled.

He is that: the unknowable, the unsearchable,

the ineffable. He is this: the revealed, the recorded, the encountered.

Had He been only the former, you and I would have had to keep silent; there would have been no talking about Him then—not, at any rate, for you and me. No, we should have had to leave it to those advanced in the practice of meditative silence and mystical contemplation. They alone would have been able to name God's name with conviction and make the word something more than an empty sound. You and I, at home in the world of flesh and matter, removed from the deep silences in which Eternity speaks, should have been awestruck, bemused, dumbfounded to hear Him even named.

Because God has chosen to be other than merely unknowable and unsearchable, we can speak of Him. You and I can bandy His name between us. You and I, undisciplined as we are in the things of the spirit, can handle with our tongue the name of Him who is from everlasting to everlasting, and yet not fear (or scarcely fear) the sudden flash of lightning or the consuming fire from an outraged heaven.

There are no condescensions more lowly, no humiliations more abject, than those of Pilate's Judgment Hall, of Gethsemane, and of Calvary. (It would be heresy to claim otherwise.) But there are divine stoopings more dismal and more drab because they are more entangled in man's commonness, in man's ordinariness. It is just such a concession to man's mediocrity that God has submitted Himself to be talked about, that God has lent Himself a subject for human chatter.

"He was there. So-and-so saw Him. He said this. He said that. I've heard that he healed a woman." That, no doubt, was how they talked of Him in the days of His life in the flesh, and there has been much more since, down the centuries. "Personally I'm sure He was there. Saint Luke says He was. Saint Matthew drops a hint. Saint Mark keeps suggestively quiet. But I've had a private word with Q. . . . " Of course we call it scholarship today, whereas then they called it gossip. No doubt there is a difference, but we must not exaggerate it.

God has submitted Himself to be ceaselessly talked about. "Professor Whosit says it all depends whether you believe Christ was just another man. [Applause] Well, you can't expect the experts here to settle that one for you at this time. [Laughter] So good night now, listeners, from the members of our team . . . "

God has submitted Himself to this sort of thing.

In a very real sense He asked for it. He entered the stream of human life; He possessed himself of a particular human body; and He consigned Himself for the rest of time to a universal human body. This is one of the continuing results of the Incarnation: He is continually talked about by anybody and everybody, and He shares that lot with the pin-up film star, the master of the Kremlin, and the latest person to testify before a Congressional Investigation Committee; He shares it, less extensively, with the local playboy and that objectionable woman down the street.

In more ways than one, God has put Himself on the tip of men's tongues: He came among men, and could hardly expect to escape their notice; He decided not to remain high and lifted up—remote in glory, worshipful but inaccessible; He decided to be a Person whom men might run into as they walked about the streets of history.

We are physical creatures, you and I, flesh and blood, linked by sense and appetite to the animal world, but, we must admit, God has given to us more than He has to any other creatures in that world, and to us He has conceded the most. The mere fact of His assuming human flesh was an immeasurable concession, but what followed that assumption was, in a sense, even more remarkable.

The Incarnation turned out to be not a means of getting in touch with us, not a device for Him to have a confidential word with us and so put us right, not even a way of *explaining* anything first-hand. It was not a matter of *telling* man, but of *being* man. He did not come primarily to correct history, but to inhabit history.

It could have been quite different, of course: He might have come with a far different purpose, such as gently but firmly to sort us all out. But the Incarnation was not an experiment in divine slumming: God did not come as some potentate to address his inferiors; He did not come to assist us philanthropically with the right contacts and the right advice; He did not come to patronize us. The ancient mythical gods of the pagans had come to earth with that kind of intention, but our Lord came here to *be*, and to be in the form of a man—to *be man,* and to endure whatever might have to be endured by Eternal God when being man—and that a full man behind whose manhood His divinity lay hidden from the world.

He not only came into the world as man, but He conceded the maximum to our animality in that He assumed manhood at the physical level instead of merely instructing it at the intellectual level. He did not deliver a course of lectures on

"The Accessibility of the Divine," nor even on "How to get in touch with God." Inhabiting a human body, he did not speak and act as though it were a concession to do so—a temporary inconvenience endured in the interest of something higher, more intellectual or spiritual, than the crude business of being a sentient biped. He did not "philosophize" His Incarnation. He did not say, "I am here among you as a man, but do not let these arms and legs deceive you; this body is a mere means to an end: do not let it preoccupy you, do not let it exhaust your attention, for it is a mere instrument for conveying to you the truth about the unseen and the intangible. You must look beyond me and my deeds to the spiritual reality which I express."

God the Son never said anything like that. He never acted as though His divine role were of that kind. Worship our Lord or reject Him, but do not look upon Him as a divine loud-speaker through which the message of the supernatural is broadcast to mankind. He is not that; He is not God's "intercom," connecting time and eternity. It is blasphemy to regard Him like that, for the essential thing about a loud-speaker is that you make the best use of it when you ignore the instrument itself and concentrate upon the sounds it brings from the invisible distance. Our Lord is not to be listened to in that way. He is to be looked at, stared at, thought about, worshipped *in Himself* and *in all His humanity.* He is not a window through which one may look upon infinite Truth and Reality. He is Himself Truth; He is Reality.*

He is all this in Himself, and in Himself as man. He is all this not merely in Himself as a teacher, a prophet, a director of souls; but in Himself as a man—a walking, gesturing, eating, drinking man. If we bow down to Him as only a *vehicle* of uttered truth and not as Truth Itself, if we kneel to Him as only an unerring spokesman whose *ex cathedra* pronouncements infallibly reveal the nature of things eternal, we misconstrue His Incarnation. He is not the supreme truth-spinner; He is supreme Truth Itself.

He is all this *in His fullness as a man.* Therefore it is not enough to worship Him simply in His capacity as a teacher with a divine message, or a healer with miraculous cures, or as a prophet with

*"MARY VIRGIN: [Watching our Lord on the way to Calvary] I know now what he is, and what I am. . . . I, Mary, am the fact; God is the truth; but Jesus is fact and truth—he is reality. . . . From the beginning of time until now, this is the only thing that has ever really happened. When you understand this you will understand all prophecies, and all history. . . ." Dorothy L. Sayers, *The Man Born to Be King* (New York: Harper & Brothers, 1949).
*The practical implications of Christian teaching about personal obedience re-explored to some length in the author's *The Will and the Way* (The Macmillan Co.).

a solemn warning. It is not enough to worship Him in His capacity as God paying a visit to His realms within time, for He came in no supervisory or exploratory capacity. Rather we must worship Him in His capacity as a man—a man with hands and legs and a face, for, when the time came, it was the hands and legs and the face which accomplished the work of salvation. True, the brain had constructed the parable, the voice had declared the mystery of the kingdom, but it was the face and the hands and the side that bled.

He suffered and died, not just to demonstrate something, but to achieve something. He bled and died, not that He might convincingly illustrate the superiority of humility over pride and of self-giving over self-seeking—though He most certainly did all of that, but He bled and died because suffering and dying were something that, in itself, had to be done. Being God and becoming man involved precisely that. It was the very nature of things in our fallen world that being God and becoming man should necessarily involve self-sacrifice. That was the kind of world it was—and still is. Let us not deceive ourselves. The Crucifixion was the consequence and the price of divinizing manhood.

Why did manhood have to be divinized? We

may ask why a patient has to receive a blood-transfusion (the analogy is tolerably instructive). Corruption had eaten away the true face and frame of humanity. Sin was destroying, as it always destroys, the very *human-ness* of man. That is the nature of evil: to take away from whatever it attacks the very quality which makes that something what it is. Evil destroys in a thing that which makes it itself. A roof with a gaping hole made by a bomb is for all practical purposes no longer a roof; it has ceased to give shelter, and the provision of shelter is the roof's *raison d'etre*. That is precisely what a roof is—a shelter over one's head; but the hole detracts from the roof's roof-ness. Sin was eating away the human-ness of humanity. Man was created to love and serve God in freedom, but he was ceasing to serve the purpose for which he was made—the thing which makes him what he is. It was necessary, therefore, to *re-humanize* man.

Only a transfusion of the *truly and uncorruptedly human* could re-humanize our race. The human was everywhere corrupted, and there was no untainted human blood available to be injected into our arteries and veins. The patient cannot cure the patient; the thief cannot reform the thief. The truly human had to be re-created, not by calling off the whole business and starting all over again, but by the injection of new and un-sullied humanity. God in heaven could have annihilated corrupt humanity and made a fresh start, but only God in man could renew corrupt humanity from within. Manhood had to be divinized in order to be rehumanized. It was necessary to re-create a family cleansed and cured within the family defaced and corrupted. The inner family must consist of men and women reborn into the new and perfect humanity fash-ioned by God Himself. The cost of the re-creation was the Crucifixion—the inevitable consequence of the divine act within the sphere of the temporal and the fallen. It was inevitable because good and evil are irreconcilably antagonistic to each other; it was the inevitable cost because there is no third course between obedience and disobedience. Man must be reborn or perish, and the Crucifixion was the only life saver.

So the divine became human: God became man. To weaken either term in these balanced sentences is to miss essential Christian truth. Our concern here is with the fullness of our Lord's humanity, and, if it is not illogical to say so, with the sheer *human-ness* of that humanity, the opaque, sub-stantial human-ness which refuses to be overlooked as an incidental. Our Lord's humanity is not an

11

instrumental one, exploited to a superhuman end; it is a plumbed humanity, an embraced humanity, a cherished, settled-in humanity. It is also a torn, squeezed out, utterly surrended humanity.

It is a humanity of flesh and blood in which God concedes the maximum to our animality. What does it mean to say that God has done that? To answer the question, we must ask another: What aspects of our human existence most crudely reflect our animal status? Thoughtful people might point to one of our natural functions—the human mode of reproduction, or to another function—the human mode of nourishing ourselves by consuming food and drink and by rejecting waste material. These two functions are not, however, on a level, and few people would wish to place them so. Indeed many (not least among unbelievers) would be outraged to see our human mode of reproduction quoted as something which reflects our animal status. "Only in a very limited sense does it do so," they would say. "Its animal quality is transfigured in human beings by the emotional and spiritual quality which accompanies sexual love and the upbringing of children."

This is true. Our mode of reproduction seems to link us in some respects with the animal world, but in other respects it is a feature of human life by which man is clearly exalted above the animal world. The sexual appetite is nowadays so entangled with disinterested love and with the highest aspirations of aesthetic culture that it is easier for our contemporaries to regard sex as a spiritualizing force than to face its potent animality. It would not be relevant here to comment on the validity or health of current attitudes toward sex, for that is not what we are considering. Rather, our point is that of the two functions which root us with animal kind in mother earth, one (the reproductive function) has been decked out with genuine romanticism (as well as with false glamor), has been refined and exalted through art, has been cleaned and spiritualized in monogamy and home making. Thus, if we are looking for evidence of our earthiness, our animality, it is not satisfactory to look primarily at our mode of reproduction, for it is precisely at that point, in the cultivation of what we may call sex-culture, that man reveals in himself most forcefully the angelic as well as the bestial.

Let us therefore consider the manner by which we nourish ourselves by consuming food and drink. Surely this links us plainly with the animal world; surely this binds us, literally binds us, to the earth. We devour the products of the earth, we dig up buried growths from the soil, we cut up and burn the insides of hogs and sheep, we warm up the hen's ova, we slice up the stale, rotting, and solidified milk of the cow. Surely here, in the daily fuelling of the body with the seed and waste and superfluity of plant and beast—surely here we touch rock bottom in our search for man's animal affiliations.

Despite gastronomes and gourmets, man the eater remains man the animal. The chewing, crunching, gulping creature is as surely linked with the animal world by his jaw work and gullet work as he is exalted above the animal world by reciting a poem or playing a violin. Our alimentary processes are as distinctly animal as our symphonies are distinctively human.

When our Lord wished to establish a sacramental act through which men might know and worship Him throughout the centuries, He fastened on food and drink as the medium. He addressed Himself to man the eater, man the drinker—not to man the thinker, man the artist, man the contemplative, but to man the consumer of food and drink.

It could have been otherwise. In that upper room on the Thursday evening a far different scene might have been enacted. Our Lord could have called for two minutes of quiet reflection on the bounty and justice of God. He might have asked for a minute of silent prayer and inner openness to the promptings of the Spirit. He might have urged His disciples to lay aside for ten minutes all thought of the temporal and to surrender themselves to mystical contemplation. He might have conducted any one of many such little ceremonies, and then said, "Do this in remembrance of me." Instead, He gave them food and drink.

Our Lord fastened on the least intellectual, the most purely animal thing we do in our daily lives and made of it His most blessed Sacrament. What a lot this reveals to us! How anxious our Lord must have been that there should be no mistake, that men should understand how He had plunged into the depth of their manhood, that men should know he was not trifling with their humanity, not skirting its obdurate earthiness, not toying fastidiously with its red-blooded animality, that they should know he was man indeed! And how far away it all is from what the sentimental idealists and the wooly-headed humanists look for to satisfy their "deep"(?) religious aspirations—how far away from the thin abstractions of philosophical religiosity and ethical uplift! What an offense to refined good taste! What a stumbling block to the cultivated intellect!

He did not say, "My spirit pervades this silence; worship it." He did not say, "My heart is open to your hearts; commune with it." He did not say, "My truth fills this tranquil quiet; contemplate it." Instead he said, "This meal is I—it is I, myself —flesh and blood. Eat it."

Our Lord most certainly reckons with our animal connections; He caters to them. During His incarnate life He healed bodies as well as souls. He fed the Five Thousand, and fed them well. He could have left them hungry—he could have taken the opportunity to point out to those who had followed Him into the wilderness that discipleship was a costly pursuit. "You have followed me to hear my words," He might have said. "And now you are hungry. That is the price of pursuing the spiritual: your bodies must be disciplined, your appetites denied. Use this fast together as an occasion for spiritual detachment from the burdensome flesh. Learn to break through the sphere of the physical to the spiritual reality beyond." That was not His way. He said, "Make the men sit down."

It is part and parcel of our Lord's assumption of our full humanity that he should have fed the hungry and healed the sick, and so catered to our basic physical needs. It is likewise in accord with

16

His assumption of our full humanity that our Lord should have made His Blessed Sacrament from the act of eating and drinking. Now, in our own day, when the Eucharist is rightly enriched with all manner of uplifting ceremony, and comes into our lives as the focus of centuries of spiritual discipline and devotion, we must never allow ourselves to evade or gloss over the mighty significance of this fact: it speaks of a God who was not content to instruct or direct man, but rather who chose to *be* man, full man, active on the inescapable earthly level on which we eat, digest, and breed, on that humbling level on which we get the toothache, develop arthritis, grow bald, sicken, and die.

Thus our Lord, through His Church, addresses us in our capacity as human beings, not as virtually disembodied spirits, not as minds with regrettable physical attachments which burden and dull them, but as full human beings invited to eat as well as to pray. It is something of a change for us these days to be addressed in that capacity. It is a novelty to be appealed to in all our widespread humanity—a refreshing novelty to the sturdier souls but a shocking one to the delicate and fastidious souls, for we are not used to it. More often, nowadays, we are appealed to as voters, taxpayers, customers, wage-earners, readers, listeners, viewers,

17

and so on. We have grown accustomed to being addressed in a limited capacity—as householders, clients, alumni, married men with one dependent relative, and whatnot. To be addressed in our full humanity is disturbingly different. The reach and range of it is so extensive that it embraces the profound mystery of our immortal longings and the crude thrust of our elemental instincts. The Church embarrasses men with her mode of address. To be invited to eat and drink by an institution (or rather a Body) which does not sell groceries—that is odd, to say the least; but since the invitation to eat and drink is conjoined with a call to worship and adore, there is, if we consider the matter, something overwhelming in the comprehensiveness of the demand. Much in us protests against this wholesale encounter with our richly blended humanity. Must the Church remind us, when we are about the comfortable task of cultivating our souls, that we have bodies too— teeth that crunch and tongues that lick? It is unnerving—similar to those sudden probing reminders of what our mortal lot is like, which we hastily brush off with a sweep of the pen: "Do you suffer from epilepsy, apoplexy, giddiness, or sleeping sickness? Answer YES or NO."

The Church's appeal to the full man is logical

and necessary. It is meet and right, for our Lord embraced not a limited humanity, not a humanity without teeth or tongue, but a full humanity. There was no deception about the Incarnation: we can be quite sure of that. God did not "dress up" as man: He did not assume a carefully conditioned flesh to hide behind the mask and mummery of expurgated manhood. He became true man.

Moreover, our Lord's humanity is a *rounded* humanity—rounded in the sense that there is nothing specialized about it. We who live in an age of excessive specialization ought to appreciate this. Of late—during the last hundred years or so —our heroes and idols have been one-sided creatures, and that is peculiarly the case today. We have come to take one-sidedness for granted. Contemporary biographies of distinguished artists, scholars, sportsmen, and statesmen suggest that we are not much interested in human all-roundedness. The outstanding gift of the gifted man so fascinates us that we pay little attention to the deficiencies of the man's personality. We categorize our great ones: the thinker, the artist, the soldier, the mystic, the man of action, and even the saint.

Our Lord cannot be categorized. Occasional attempts have been made to do so, but they have failed. The nineteenth century created the Gentle-

Jesus-meek-and-mild image, but it has not endured. An image built solely on the picture of the Good Shepherd, the friend of little children, and on a few selected exhortations from what is commonly called the "Sermon on the Mount," proves ludicrously incongruous with the picture we see when we read about the Pharisees and His hounding of the money changers. At times in our Lord's incarnate life we see that great ascetic and recluse, then we see a sociable healer, rubbing shoulders with the mob; at one moment He is the with-drawn visionary, and at the next He is the acclaimed idol of the masses. Here He is the confidential instructor of a small band of followers; there He is the popularizer—a story teller for the crowd.

It is important for us to realize that we cannot label our Lord's interests and activities as predominantly intellectual, or social, or practical, or philanthropic. Although He taught earnestly and convincingly, He did not cultivate His hearers' minds so exclusively that He could be accused of a bias towards intellectual interests. Although He made the sick well and restored the dead to life, and although he sought to bring comfort to the poor and the underprivileged, no one could charge Him with an excessive bias in favor of mere physical well-being. He urged compassion, charity, mercy, and sympathy, but it would be absurd, as well as blasphemous, to pretend to see in the figure of our Lord a disproportionate over-balance of the tenderer sensibilities. His humanity is utterly without favor towards the intellectual, the physical, or the emotional. There is no hint of too much sophistication here or too much feel-ing there, too little reflection on this occasion or too ready an indulgence on that. As we study Him, His fullness becomes clearer and surer.

His humanity is a complete and rounded humanity. The divinity which dwells in it reaches into every corner of human experience. If we are reborn into our Lord's humanity, we are reborn into a balanced humanity. Above all, there is nothing in our Lord's teaching, character, or actions to suggest an evasion of the physical. His is a story of bodies healed and mouths fed; a story in which bread and fish and wine play a larger part than any intellectual abstractions. There is blood, tears, sweat, and a gashed side. We have been allowed, if not encouraged, to charge the thinker, the teacher, the prophet, and the "leader" with a bias towards what we call the theoretical— the ideal, the abstract. In those who are profound in judgment and wise in understanding, we detect (or think we detect) an evasion of life's earthier and homelier aspects. There is nothing of the sort in our Lord.

2

DOUBLE-VISION

GOD's full acceptance of humanity in the Incarnation demands from men the full recognition of our Lord's divinity. Jesus is God and man: divinity is incarnate in Him, and humanity is divinized in Him. That has always been the teaching of the Church. Throughout the ages heresy about the nature of our Lord has been based upon neglect of one or the other of these balanced and fully blended truths. We must bear in mind that the proper understanding of the true nature of our Lord is by no means a purely theoretical matter: on the contrary, it is an intensely practical matter; for in the person and acts of our Lord we see, and see concretely, what God does with humanity—and that is something we need to know, for we all have a humanity to offer Him. Because of our imperfections, and because we always hold something back, the offering of our humanity is inadequate and incomplete; but our Lord's humanity was totally given, and in Him we can see what God does with humanity when He gets a free hand with it. In possessing it wholly, He sanctifies every sense and every faculty: thus possessed, it is operative only at the will of God. A human voice, a human tongue, and a human hand are in action, but they carry the divine word, the divine forgiveness, the healing touch of God.

Our Lord's humanity was wholly given to God throughout His life: hence His teaching, ministering, succouring, and healing were totally fruitful. Our Lord's humanity was also wholly given to God in death: hence His death was a full and perfect sacrifice. One strains after images, in the hope of expressing with some vividness and concreteness what this means, but it is as though God gave our humanity like a robe to His Son and said, "Clean this." The Son wore that humanity—He wore it and washed it in the water of active and sinless earthly experience; then, in suffering and death, He wrung it out dry and gave it back to the Father. The same robe is put upon us at our Baptism. Thus, through our membership in the Church, the Body of Christ, our humanity is renewed, perfected, and offered.

The assumption by God of our humanity gives to that humanity a status and a value which it would not otherwise have had. In the same way, God's entry into our time and space gives to the things of this life—the earthly environment itself —a significance which they would not otherwise have had. The Doctrine of the Incarnation thus corroborates, enriches, and extends certain truths already implicit in the Doctrine of Divine Creation. The Doctrine of Creation tells us that this world and the creatures dwelling in it are in themselves good things—they *must* be good since God created them, for presumably God is a successful creator and not a botcher. It would be nonsensical to regard Him as a creator whose work did not quite come off, or whose creation proved to be a failure: a successful creator is one who creates what he sets out to create.

To say that the creatures dwelling in this world are in themselves good things is not by any means to praise them or to applaud them; rather it is to praise their Creator. That is to say, it is better that men and women should exist—even with their shocking deficiences—than that they should not exist. To agree that the creation of human beings was worthwhile, does not hinder one from admitting that, by and large, they have made an ugly mess of what they inescapably are—two-legged creatures with brains and senses and immortal souls; to say that men and women are in themselves good things is not to deny that all of them, individually, may be wicked sinners. When we claim that everything made by God is good, and that human beings come into this category, it is like saying that the theatre is a good thing: the theatre would remain *in itself* an essentially good thing even if all the theatres in the world started to put on nothing but salacious and immoral shows. When something of the sort actually happened in England, during the Restoration period, puritan critics cried out, "You see, the theatre is a wicked and ungodly thing. Let abolish it." The theatre in itself was not at fault: it was the abuse of the theatre. We must always distinguish between a thing in itself and the abuse or perversion of that thing. If, for instance, all the hopsitals in the world became so corrupted that their staffs started to poison their patients in the interest of administrative convenience and general comfort all around, that tragic state of affairs would not prove hospitals *in themselves* to be bad things. If a disaster of that kind occurred, the proper thing to do would be, not to abolish all hospitals, but to clean them up. The baby should not be thrown out with the bathwater.

The doctrine that God created men implies that men, as sentient, rational, living bipeds, are in themselves good things. By being what they essentially and inescapably are—alive, with appetities and aspirations and consciences, with moral freedom and capacity to love—they represent something which God wanted to exist.

The Doctrine of Creation applies not only to the beings who inhabit the earth but also to the world itself; thus the value of the whole world is similarly assured. We may logically assume that just as any artist will strive to put into his work qualities of which he approves, and that as any truly great artist will be successful in his attempt, so God Himself must have put into the whole creation qualities of which He approves. (The only alternative is to claim that God's creative workmanship has been faulty.) It follows that when we are looking with perceptions and responses unspoiled by any kind of passion or ignorance, what we see in the natural world will probably manifest qualities approved of by the world's Maker. It may be, of course, that few of us are capable of looking at the objective world with a full vision and with a mind cleared of corrupting forces of prejudice and egotism. Nevertheless, most of us, at some time or other in our lives, must have responded with momentary awe to the spectacle of some moving or magnificent loveliness in the land or the sea or the sky. In doing so—in catching a glimpse of the full beauty in which God chose to invest the natural order, we sense what kind of workman He is and what kind of thing He considers worth making.

The Doctrine of the Incarnation, we have said, corroborates, enriches, and extends truths already implicit in the Doctrine of Creation: thus God's assumption of our humanity and His entry into our earthly environment reinforce the knowledge that our manhood and our world are alike intensely worthwhile. We have a humanity which was not only made by God, but also indwelt and redeemed by God. He thought it worth inhabiting and worth saving—whatever the cost. Arms and legs, eyes and brain—all the properties of our humanity were assumed by God, used by Him, offered up by Him. Moreover, we have, as the physical background to our lives, an earthly environment which was not only made by God, but also inhabited by Him. He thought it worth visiting and living in. Flowers and fields and cities were praised and trodden and wept over. Our human life in time and place—now, and on this planet—is dear because the whole was built by the mind and hand of God. It is dearer still because its fullness and its brevity, its stretch and its limitations, have been enjoyed and endured by the Incarnate God.

This means that we cannot write off the human against the divine, the temporal against the eternal, the earthly against the heavenly, in a series of contrasts or antagonisms. It means that we cannot construct a balance sheet of earthly experience, with the physical listed under "liabilities" and the spiritual counted as "assets." It means that we cannot tolerate a notion of life which divorces the secular and the religious. It means that we cannot deny God an entry into the most hidden and remote corners of human experience. Conversely, we cannot deny to the most trivial thing a possible place in shaping here and now what is eternally meaningful.

Catholic teaching trains us to look out upon the whole field of human experience with a kind of double vision. We have to look at all things two ways. We face our fellows and our environment in a double capacity: our fellows and their environment likewise exist in a double capacity too. We are creatures of time but also pilgrims of eternity, sons of Adam but also reborn in Christ, children of nature but also sons of God. It is disastrous, indeed fatal, when men try to live as though they were only the one or only the other. The double vision is essential to sanity and sanctity. The Doctrine of the Incarnation is the fountain and archetype of all double sight and double understanding—of *full* sight and *whole* understanding. Our Lord is both God and man. Divinity is incarnate in Him; humanity is divinized in Him. Our theological thinking (if it is sound) and our ecclesiastical practice (if it is Catholic) reflect and recapitulate that balance, that tension, that duality—indeed, that fullness, that wholeness.

That there is tension as well as balance need not surprise us and ought not upset us. (Its fuller implications will be dealt with at a later point in this book.) Double vision is necessary to a proper conception of the Church, for the Church is, at one and the same time, a human institution turned Godward and the Divine Body turned manward: it is the fellowship of worshiping, dependent, frail creatures of dust, but at the same time it is the mystical Body of Christ on earth. It is a tainted society of fumbling and sinful creatures, yet it is also the band of God's elect, gathered, and regenerate. Catholic orthodoxy holds in balance the temporal and the eternal views of the Church, whereas heresy destroys the balance by weakening or ignoring one or the other of the two blended truths. Christians dominated by extreme quietism or antinomianism have tried to conceive of the Church only in its eternal aspect. Fanatically obsessed with distorted notions of grace or election, seventeenth-century schismatics, like the Molinists in Spain and the Familists in England, overlooked their temporal responsibilities and their duties to their fellow men. They were prepared to sacrifice morality and common sense in the cultivation of an imaginary mystical exclusiveness. That is an extreme, although no longer fashionable. For the twentieth century, the heresy, generally speaking, is quite the opposite—the neglect of the Church as the Divine Body. Far too many of our contemporaries see the Church only in its temporal aspect; to them the Church is only a collection of human beings who in fellowship are seeking a divine blessing on their otherwise earthbound activities. That, too, is an extreme, and one that accounts for much of today's sentimental humanism which passes for, but is not, Christianity.

The balance between contrary emphases maintained in the traditional doctrine of the Church is characteristic of Catholic thinking generally. Our faith fully reckons with the duality of the human situation—the basic conception of a finite order existing in the hands of an infinite God; it reckons with the now as well as the then, with the is and the ought-to-be, with the finite and the infinite, with time and with eternity. We see the duality pushed to its furthermost and extreme limits when we contemplate the God-man-hood of our Lord—the crucified Nazarene as Eternal God sacrificed for man. The same double vision operates in instances far less momentous: it enables us, for example, to see a flower both as the product of seed and soil and sun, and at the same time as the handiwork of God. In all things our faith teaches us to remember simultaneously the two different modes under which things exist:—things and people and events, all that has being and all that transpires at our side *within nature* and *under God*. Catholic doctrine (and more especially the Doctrine of the Incarnation, with its numerous implications) has not done its work with us, and Catholic practice has not done its work with us, until the influence of each has developed in us the capacity to comprehend objects, experiences, and persons under the two different aspects, within nature and under God, at the same time.

Consider, for instance, human flesh and the life of the senses, To the puritan, who is insensitive to sacramental thinking, the flesh is a thing of nature, corrupted and corrupting. To the modern secular humanist who, by contrast, frequently seasons his time-locked philosophy with a dash of pagan romanticism, the flesh and its appetites have a peculiar "unearthly" glamour and become in themselves a source of value; in particular the sexual appetite is given a pseudo-religious status, and marital, filial, and parental obligations must bow before it. For the Catholic, however, the human flesh is both a thing of nature, subject to corruption, and a thing transfigurable, once inhabited by our Lord. The experience of the senses, pursued for its own sake only, is lawlessness and death; the experience of the senses, offered to God and disciplined by His Church, is a means to joy and peace, even to sanity and sanctity.

It is true to say that, in so far as we move from the central doctrines of the Church to investigate the various emphases of the sects, we shall find, in one way or another, a weakening or an abandonment of double vision. For instance, the Churchman has no difficulty in regarding the Bible as very truly God's word and, at the same time, the immediate product of human intelligence; we have no difficulty at all in accepting the theological truth of the book of Genesis alongside its historical naivetes and scientific untruths. Fundamentalists, however, see the Bible under the single aspect, as the inspired word of God only, and therefore *literally* infallible. On the other hand, skeptics see the Bible under the converse aspect, as nothing more than the product of scientifically uninformed human thought. Furthermore, the Churchman sees his parish priest not only as a man like himself, a person with whom he can have ordinary human dealings, but also, and at the same time, as a priest of God's Church, empowered by the authority of his office to forgive sins and administer the sacraments. The sectarian simply will not recognize the combination of person and office in one individual: in his literalness he regards the claim to priestly authority as a personal matter, if not assumption; when in truth it is an institutional and indelible fact. (Conversely, those in the Church can make a similar, and more dangerous, mistake by confusing the dignity of the office with, say, the humility of the person.)

The blessing of double vision—of seeing things under two different aspects—is especially significant in relation to the Church's sacraments, for upon the Doctrine of the Incarnation the Church has built a system of intercourse between God and man which richly answers human need and which is perfectly in accord with what our Lord taught and did. Sacraments by their very nature have an ambivalent quality. In the Eucharist the bread and wine become the Body and Blood, and yet they remain bread and wine also. We have already stressed that the Eucharist, built as it is upon the function of eating and drinking, goes to the extremities of man's manhood and pulls his humanity up to the divine; it is equally important that by using the simplest of earth's products as the vehicles of the Real Presence, the Eucharist goes to the heart of nature and raises that also to the divine.

That is why it is inadequate to think of the Eucharist as only a means of grace (important though that aspect is), or only as a felicitously devised means of worship. In truth the Eucharist is something far more than a means—even more than a means of sacrifice and oblation. It is wrong to assign to the elements, the bread and the wine, a merely *instrumental* character or function, for the act of communion is not a means of giving physical expression to something spiritual: it is neither a mere means nor a mere device. The shaking of hands is a formal and conventional device to express friendship and good will, but it is by no means universal since there are regions where the rubbing of noses takes its place. The elements are not merely instrumental; they are *symptomatic*. The connection between the outward and physical and the inward and spiritual is not an ordinary or conventional connection: it is a *significant* connection. It is more like the connection between a smile and a cheerful spirit—a connection inherent in our very nature—than the artificial link between, say, tipping one's hat and feeling respect for womanhood.

The significance of the connection between the form and the meaning of the Eucharist has three especially relevant aspects: that wheat and grapes are products of the natural world indicates how the whole of creation is brought into the sphere of sanctification; that bread and wine are the products of man's skill shows how all of man's healthy labor (and all that is truly valuable in man's civilization) is brought into the same sphere of sanctification; that the act of communion is to eat and to drink draws the full range of man's physical life into that same sphere. It is by eating and drinking that our bodies are nourished, that we grow, and that we survive; and this process, essential to survival, provides the only adequate outward form for the act of receiving spiritual nourishment, the act of partaking of the Divine Life.

The connection between the bread and wine and the Body and Blood of our Lord is not, then, a conventional or, let us say, a contrived one; nor is it a product of fancy or caprice. Our Lord's choice of bread and wine is not at all what aesthetic critics might call a "highly imaginative touch": it is a profound choice. Christ deliberately and purposefully chose them not only to express divine sacrifice, but also, and in respect of the whole natural order, to *signify* something. The Eucharist is, in this aspect, an epitome of the true Christian life: in it man gives praise to God, affirms his faith, repents his sins, offers himself in union with the perfect sacrifice of our Lord, and feeds on the food of eternal life. The blending, at the supreme moment, of the natural (the wheat and the grape) and the humanly physical (eating and drinking) with the divine, represents the true pattern of human experience. The double vision by which we are enabled to see together and at once the natural and the supernatural, the temporal and the eternal, the physical and the spiritual, is something which we must carry over into every field of our earthly life.

During the last few years we have heard a great deal (too much, in fact) about the "Christian view" of this and the "Christian view" of that— so much that we are sometimes tempted to regret that the word "Christian" ever became an adjective; but surely, if there can be a "Christian view" of anything, it must be precisely this: a view which holds a thing simultaneously in its temporal and in its eternal aspects. If there is a "Christian way" of looking at human beings and their doings, it must surely be that of consistently seeing them both *in nature* and *under God*. To say this has never been more necessary than now, when the "Christian view" of politics, education, and the like, turns out to be, in the eyes of many, little more than a "frame of mind"—an approach to any field of human activity that is based on the idea that there is one God and that behavior counts for something, at least amongst our neighbors.

Double vision—the "Christian view"—is essential to the understanding of life, for it operates over the largest fields of public events as well as in the most intimate spheres of personal experience. The Christian is conscious of the activity of divine Providence when he surveys the great movements and events of contemporary affairs or when he studies the developments and disasters in human history. It is presumptuous, no doubt, to try to trace in too fine and exact detail the workings of God's hand in affairs of the world, but it is utter unbelief to be totally blind to His activity. The Christian can scarcely reflect upon the career of a Hitler without sensing the power of preternatural evil lurking in the universe, and without recognizing the pattern of its dominion over the human soul. Nor can the Christian reflect upon the career

38

of a Schweitzer or an Abbe Pierre without noting gratefully and humbly how the hand of God raises up men equal to the encroachments of suffering and distress. In this respect we should notice that Christians of strong evangelical conviction have often been especially wise and sensitive in applying double vision, as it should be applied, to human history and to contemporary affairs. We all can learn from them. We must see the events of history, its great movements, turning points, developments, and disasters, on two levels at once; see events knit together in a pattern of causation, formed under the influence of earthly environment and earthly accident, of human impulse and human desire; and see the same events woven into a larger pattern that shows the masterful handiwork of God. Divine Providence is certainly at work in history, and wherever and whenever the hand of God is at work on earth, there and then men's eyes must be watchful, their minds alert, and their ears attentive. God is a tireless teachers: we have only to watch and listen.

Especially is this true of our private lives, for therein is an even more imperative demand to cultivate double vision. We must be prepared to see our Christian acquaintances as fellow citizens and children of God too. We must never forget that however we are here employed we ourselves have a prior allegiance to another world. We must be perpetually alert to discerning God's designs for us in the joys He sends to delight us and the disappointments sent to discipline us. In respect to ourselves—to knowing ourselves, to helping ourselves—the enjoyment of a healthy spiritual life depends on double vision. It is essential, utterly necessary, in our Christian pilgrimage that we should learn to know ourselves, in all our squalid and yet divine duplicity, for what we actually are —fallen sinners, unfit even to plead for mercy, but still God's own redeemed children, called to eat at His table.

Finally we may observe that the whole of the Church's practice in worship and observance presupposes the fruitful operation of the Christian double vision. Her ritual is necessarily unacceptable to those who see the temporal and the eternal, the physical and the spiritual, in conflict and opposition. The truth is that the ritual brings the physical into harmony with the spiritual, for the body is allowed to offer its homage in its own way. The Christian believes that the Incarnation has made double vision essential to Christian outlook. It is pre-eminently the Christian mode of response to, and reflection upon, the human environment, to see things *in nature* and to see them *under* God. If we are thoughtful and logical, this mode of thinking will extend itself over an ever-widening field of objects and events, actions and persons. In the eyes of the enlightened, there is no uncorrupted thing so trivial that the weight of God's presence cannot be imprinted upon it as symbol or sacrament, and there is no created thing so cheap that it cannot bear a part in the praise of its Maker.

3

OUR OWN OFFERING

THE argument of this book so far may be summed up as follows. By the pattern of our Lord's incarnation and self-offering, and by the teaching and practice of the Church, we are committed, as Christians, to a distinctive kind of life. This life, the specifically Christian one, is that in which the spiritual explores the full stretch of the physical and the intellectual; a life in which the full range of the human is visited by God; a life in which the products of nature and of human effort are offered to Him. Thus the divine and the human, the eternal and the temporal, meet at every point in the fully Christian pilgrimage. It follows therefore that, if we are to achieve a way of life consonant with our Christian profession, we must cultivate that double vision by which openness to the supernatural is habitually conjoined with awareness of the natural.

It is now time to explore some of the practical implications of these general truths. We note first that our Lord's assumption and sanctification of a full humanity carries the implication that we, as Christians, are not to evade our humanity, either physically or spiritually. There are many ways in which we Christians are tempted to side-step the responsibilities of our full humanity, even in matters specifically religious. If our religious acts and observances do not truly constitute an offering of our full humanity, our lives will be sadly, perhaps tragically, impoverished. There is no such thing as piece-meal tribute to God. If we try, for instance, to give our brains to the things of God while our wills remain wholly our own, wholly unregenerate, our offering is like the kiss of Judas. Temptations to make an inadequate, truncated offering of ourselves assail us in specious and devious ways: in each of them the Devil attempts to put our humanity so greatly out of joint that it is utterly useless in the hands of God; if he cannot prevent us, in our wretchedness, from calling "Lord, Lord," he will certainly do his best to see that we offer up a humanity so mutilated, so fragmentary, that God can do nothing with it.

Consider, for the moment, some of the ways in which we may evade the offering of our full humanity while, paradoxically, paying a great deal of attention to religious matters. We can make our religion wholly, or predominantly, an intellec-

43

tual matter or a purely spiritual thing. We can cultivate an exclusively moral or a largely emotional religious life. It is even possible for us to make our religion a purely physical thing—a matter of movements and acts of the body, and little else. In short, there is the danger of allowing the brain, or the soul, or the will, or the emotions, or even the body, so to predominate in our supposedly religious activity that the balance proper to a fully human offering is completely lost.

How do we know when a religious life suffers from an overbalance of purely intellectual activity? What kind of life and personality does it produce? It is a life in which plenty of time is spent in reading about religion, or talking about religion, arguing in discussion groups, or following current religious controversies, but in which there is a gross neglect of prayer, meditation, sacraments, self-discipline, and good works. It is important to note that the temptations of intellectualized Christianity, pernicious as they are, assail men and women of all classes and at different levels of intelligence, but are perhaps most dangerous to the men and women who are engaged professionally in intellectual occupations.

Thus it is possible for the scholarly theologian, immersed in his latest piece of research, or preoccupied with his latest book, to destroy his own religious life at the very time he is concentrating on religious issues. It is indeed a grave and tragic possibility, yet it is so ironical and so grotesque as to be almost comic. "I'll spend another hour on this chapter tonight. I can miss my prayers and meditation for once. After all, this is a religious book that I'm writing." It is indeed a religious book, and the chapter he is working on is headed, "The Life of Prayer." A priest may say, "I can't possibly see Mr. Jones this week. Every minute is taken, and I've just got to finish my article for *Theology*. I'm sorry if he's in a bad way, but a promise is a promise and I've got to stick to it." Mr. Jones is left without attention, but the article, titled "Contemporary Demands of Charity," is turned out on time.

Every branch of religious studies—biblical, historical, theological, liturgical, and biographical—has its own fascination for the brain—a fascination which *in itself* is neither more nor less sacred than the fascination of nuclear physics or comparative anatomy. In so far as the pursuit of religious studies is a mere delight of the brain and a satisfaction of the assertive and acquisitive ego, it has no religious quality or significance at all. It may be as much a distraction from the truly religious duties of life as the next man's passion for crossword puzzles or bridge.

We must not imply, however, that cerebral religion is found only among the learned: its temptations attack all who find any kind of intellectual pleasure in religious matters whatever they be—doctrine, ritual, ecclesiastical administration, or ecclesiastical gossip. If teachers of theology and writers of religious books can claim special knowledge of this temptation, there is no doubt that delegates to diocesan conventions and members of the altar guild have a nodding acquaintance with it too. At any rate, we must bear in mind that to bring amateur liturgiology into the office at a coffee break, or to bring the latest gossip about ecclesiastical appointments into the shower room after a round of golf, is not the same thing at all as to allow truly spiritual interests to permeate our daily activities.

There are two good reasons why the temptations to what I have called "intellectualized religion" should be especially strong and widespread in Churches of the Anglican Communion. The first (and here I am speaking rather generally) is that our Churches, and the Church of England in particular, have always been rich in scholarship and we have never depreciated the life of the intellect. We are proud of this fact. A long line of theologians, historians, commentators, philosophers, and thinkers have contributed to build up the literature of "Anglican scholarship" which is known all over Christendom for its excellence. Scholarship has been, and is, a lively thing in our Church; it earns status, respect, and preferment. We have not always been kind to our saints, and we have often ignored our prophets, but we have looked after our scholars. As a result, the latter have tasted the temptation of success, and aspirants to scholarship have tasted the temptation of ambition.

Another reason for the besetting temptation to cerebral religion is that the comprehensiveness of the Anglican Communion and the curious freedom in matters of doctrine and practice, have produced a variety of "schools" and emphases within the several Churches. When belief and practice vary, controversy is inevitable. Issues which the Church of Rome would settle with some promptness and firmness are, among us, kept alive, and all of us who take our Churchmanship seriously are offered the opportunity to join an axe-grinding "school." Just as there is some fascination in watching a tennis ball go this way and that way, so there is some fascination in observing within the Church trends towards authoritarianism or individualism, fundamentalism or liberalism, the traditional or the modern—in scoring one's opponents, and above all in acquiring and exploiting that secret vocabulary and idiom known only to the initiates of that group to which our allegiance is given. How clever to be able, with only a slight raising of the eyebrow or a slight inflection in the voice, to imply so much about the "Churchmanship" of the newly arrived priest!

But we drift into moral exhortation, and that was scarcely our aim at this point. Perilous as may be the pride and complacency and hypocrisy manifested in attitudes of this kind, we are more concerned here with the fact that they represent a confinement of religious activity to the cerebral level, and thus a truncation of the humanity which we offer to God. There is plenty of *talk* about things ecclesiastical, plenty of *thought* given to doctrine and practice, but such talk and thought by-pass the will (the spring of moral action) and are unsupported by any spiritual exercises or self-disciplines. All that happens, happens in the head. D. H. Lawrence warned us—and wisely—against sex-in-the-head. We need today a prophet as shocking and vociferous to warn us of the dangers of God-in-the-head. It is so easy to keep God there; it is so interesting, so satisfying to keep Him there; and it is often quite profitable to keep God in the head.

We need to be watchful in this matter: watchful because of the insidious ease with which a healthy and wholly human activity can be perverted into an exclusively intellectual interest. We set out, perhaps, to act as servers in God's sanctuary, in a spirit of disciplined obedience which involves the sanctifying of the whole man: but the Devil does his best to corrupt our total offering and pervert it into a merely intellectual interest in questions of ceremony and usage. Unless we are rigorous in self-examination and humble in seeking spiritual guidance, we shall scarcely observe the furtive process by which the resolution of the will crumbles and the impulse to service disintegrates, while a restless obsession with the minutiae of ritual dominates the brain, an obsession which grows fat on self-reference and in turn inflates the assertive self. This obsession, *in itself*, is of course neither more nor less unhealthy than the fanatical philatelist's obsession with stamps. It is the same sort of thing—a hobby, an intellectual hobby, an interesting exercise of the brain.

We have taken service in the sanctuary as our example, but there are of course a great many Church-centered activities which, by the same process, can be transformed into exclusively cerebral interests. For some people, clergy and laity alike, the temptation arises through participation in parochial or diocesan affairs—in committees, councils, and campaigns; others face it in their individual and passionate pursuit of the truth. This temptation can be especially acute where there is a genuine intellectual enthusiasm for the synthesis which is acquired by rational exploration of the doctrinal truths basic to our faith, for in the synthesis we find an interpretation of life's purpose and meaning which answers the questions of philosophers and thinkers. It brings danger, as well as comfort, to the intellectual. There is a hidden point at which humble, creaturely devotion to the truth slides over into possessive intellectual self-satisfaction. The thing sought for by the hungry man has become the exclusive food of the devouring brain. Let us not be misled by the use of the words "intellectual" and "brain," for the danger we are discussing here is not confined to scholars and highbrows. It is possible that the learned commentator on Corinthians I, known throughout the world for his scholarship, may have become so intellectually obsessed with textual and historical matters that the message of Saint Paul has died within him and his humanity has shrunk to the stature of a chattering encyclopaedia. It is equally possible that the secretary of the local guild of Churchwomen, known throughout the town for her interest in her fellow-creatures, may have become so obsessed with fact gathering about this person and the other, that active charity and sympathy have shrivelled into meaningless tittle-tattle. Not one of us is free from temptations of this kind.

A second way in which we can evade the responsibilities of our full humanity is by trying to make our religion an exclusively spiritual matter. In so doing we offer up to God only a useless fragment of a dismembered humanity. This may not be so notable a danger for us today, for every age has its own predominant weaknesses. In twentieth-century English speaking countries one is more likely to pervert the Christian religion into mental acrobatics, learned or trivial, than to transform it into an escapist mysticism. There is not much evidence of fanatical spiritual culture in the air, and the dangers of an obsession with the life of the soul, which by-passes the world of solid objects and living creatures, are more apparent in the eastern than in the western hemisphere. For all that, the temptations to a lop-sided cultivation of the spirit are evidenced wherever men try too rigidly to separate worship, prayer, and meditation from the life of the body and of the intellect, or from the life and work of society at large.

We tread on difficult ground here; for we can scarcely point out the dangers inherent in an unbalanced cultivation of the spirit without referring to false emphases seen in current religious groups and bodies: nevertheless we must say that any spiritual enthusiasm which demands the mutilation (as opposed to the free surrender) of mind, or body, or will is questionable. In one respect, that is our difference with Rome, and, more obviously, our difference with the fundamentalists. A fundamentalist dogmatism which requires the intellect to be gagged and blinded can never fully represent the religion of the Incarnation. It is certainly not our business to offer to God a truncated humanity; certainly not our business to strangle or smother our reason and then present Him with a tattered, maimed humanity. A humanity thus mangled is useless to God—and useless to man. One can scarcely speak too seriously on this matter at a time when an irrational biblical fundamentalism is eating into the religion of the Incarnation like a cancer. To discipline the human reason is as much a Christian duty as to discipline the human body. To mutilate or murder the human reason is perhaps as grave a dereliction of Christian duty as to mutilate or murder the human body. To murder human reason in the name of a 969-year-old Methuselah is perhaps more blasphemous than to murder it in the name of Marx or Lenin. Moreover, suicide is a mortal sin.

Apart from this particular phenomenon, we may readily admit that the cultivation of the spirit, sealed off without access to the life of the senses or the brain, and in total disregard of the life of society at large, is not a dominant or besetting error of our age. In the twentieth century the greater danger is not in the exclusive cultivation of the spirit, but rather in the total neglect of it. It is one of our especial dangers today that by continually relating religious duty to moral, humanitarian, and social issues—all to the neglect of worship, prayer, and meditation, done solely to God's glory and without earthly aims, or private or altruistic motives—we may weaken the fundamental other-worldliness of our faith.

"Sunday-only Christianity" has been ridiculed enough, and there is no need to whip a dying horse. Men and women who are cultivating their souls while allowing the springs of compassion and charity to dry up and the demands for action to be ignored, are probably more often found in sermons than in fact. We may observe, however, that the Catholic way, with its emphasis upon the sacraments and upon the homage of the body as an accompaniment to the homage of the soul, provides safeguards against a lop-sided spiritual religious life. Catholic practice nourishes in us that double vision by which the human is fully involved with the supernatural. And we may note in passing that objections to Catholic practice invariably express the lop-sided intention to exhume the spiritual from the earthly depths in which our Lord buried it, and to unravel the divine from the human pattern into which our Lord wove it.

A third way in which we may evade the responsibilities of our full humanity and lay a blemished offering at God's feet is by making our religion an exclusively moral matter. If there is a specifically "Anglican" weakness in the sphere of religion, it is no doubt the habit, if not the disease, of reducing religion to ethics. It is a prosaic failing, a dull failing, and, one may say, a "vulgar" failing. Vulgar because it takes a thing that reaches to heaven and hell, a thing that stretches out through mystery to eternity, and makes of it a set of rules on a membership card of respectable human society. Vulgar—mean even—because it looks at Almighty God inhabiting human form and treading the route from manger to cross, and can find nothing more disinterested, nothing more awesome to say than, "What guidance for the regulation of my conduct can I get from that?" Vulgar because it closes its eyes to majesty and mystery, and fastens its attention exclusively on the conduct and decorum of the temporal self.

"Christianity" deprived of its supernatural orientation is indeed a vulgar thing. The word *vulgar* (common, ordinary, sometimes profane and obscene) is used for a very good reason. The substitution of man-centered ethics for God-centered faith is a common ailment of our social and intellectual elite; and because it is so frequently a disease of our leaders and teachers, society at large is infected. We have expensive schools to disseminate the disease. The symptoms are readily recognizable. Our Lord is praised, quoted, talked about, referred to as an example; what He did and what He said are held up before us to stimulate and to guide; but the numinous, the mystery, the heights and the depths are squeezed out of the Christian faith, and we are left with a drab code that could appeal only to half-men. We must fight this disease, for it is deadly to our holy religion. When the Gospel narratives are handled like Aesop's Fables or the stories of Brer Rabbit, when the tenderest compassions and most agonizing ordeals of God-in-Man are put on a level with instructive anecdotes about binding the lion or belling the cat, moral didacticism has toppled over into blasphemy. The revelation of God-in-Man was not designed to equip earthbound men and women with a book of etiquette calculated to secure a tolerably smooth progress through time. Our religion is not a system of character building, a program for the cultivation of creditable self-esteem.

A "Christianity" which exclusively nurtures the assertive will in propriety of behavior is a Christianity anesthetized. To use the truths of our blessed religion simply as material for moulding choice specimens of moral humanity is to petrify the living faith. We are called to worship, to bow, to repent, to believe, to obey, to love, to serve. All those things first—and they must remain first. Moral improvement will result from them, for moral improvement in ourselves is God's work; to attempt to make it our own achievement is to pervert obedience into pride. Yet the attempt is made, advertised and encouraged, in print and on the air, in school and in halls, where the word of God is proclaimed as primarily a stimulus to self-improvement, or as a challenge to the already inflated ego to make itself bigger and better. The Church is a worshipping Body—alive in Christ.

56

In other words, its members are grounding their daily lives in that which is beyond and above this world—in the eternal love and energy of God. To focus attention primarily or exclusively upon the human being's individuality and in its finite framework is the very antithesis of Christian duty —and that is precisely what we do, when we turn our religion into a mere device for moulding finite individualities to a covetable moral pattern. The aims of character building, especially as known in the most expensive sector of modern education, are more often than not wholly centered on notions of worldly well-being—*men's sana in corpore sano,* a sound mind in a sound body. Such essentially self-assertive and self-centered notions are in direct conflict with the Christian call to humility and self-surrender. The conscious cultivation of an ideal self, so long as it is the object of pride and achievement, may be as pernicious an aim as the fanatical pursuit of power or wealth. When the Christian revelation is dragged in only to provide fuel and inspiration for an ethical self-culture—a culture which never reaches out of time and never transcends the interest of well-being, we have nothing more than a ghastly and diabolical perversion.

Our Lord is the Way, the Truth, and the Life.

Have we realized what that means? The Way—
not the signpost; the Truth—not the textbook;
the Life—not the tonic.

When we pray, do we, as we should, offer ourselves to God with the prayer that He will use us
to His good purposes, mould us to His pattern?
Or do we ask Him for a little supernatural contribution towards our own heroic exercise in character building? Do we bow to Him as creatures
of nothingness, unable even to lift a finger except
with His permission? Do we beg to be made, if
possible, into something usable, expendable in His
service? Or do we tell Him rather politely that
we need just a little extra help in our job of con-
structing a really decent upstanding self? Do we
surrender ourselves to God? Or do we seek His
support for the undertaking of our own individual
will? Even though the will may be bent on self-
improvement, it is still not the Christian way.
The Christian way is the total way—the total surrender of the will: even of that will which is set
on manufacturing a virtuous self garnished with
all manner of altruism and righteousness.

Never, never forget our Lord's ferocity against
the pharisees.

We have spoken of lop-sided cultivation of the
intellect, of the spirit, and of the assertive will,

but there is a fourth, and equally perilous, imbalance in the exclusively or predominantly emotional life—still in the religious sphere of things: it is the temptation to use Christian teaching and observances as mere stimuli for emotional satisfactions, and it is especially strong in those restless, bubbling extraverts whose emotions generally lie near the surface of their personalities. They are the people who smile readily and even weep readily, and they just as readily excite a sympathetic response. Often they have an engaging frankness which easily wins confidence and trust. When they are truly guileless, they can be especially companionable. When they take advantage of their surface ebullience and likeability to construct another and more calculating and hidden self, they can be disjointed personalities indeed. Be that as it may, they are the people who are easily moved by the simplest formalities of public worship, by the most obvious rhetorical cadences in prayer and sermons, and by the most superficial poetic and musical effects in hymns. For such men and women, public worship can no doubt make a satisfying appeal to the emotions—and there is nothing wrong with that, of course, provided the emotional satisfactions are not cultivated to the exclusion of interests which touch the intellect and the will.

With the people we are here considering, the emotional life is thinly spread: there are no great heights and depths, no rare ecstasies, no inner agonies. The world's poets and artists do not come from among their ranks: nor do the world's neurotics and lunatics. They do not have nervous breakdowns. They are seldom free from surface emotions, but their disturbances are rarely deep.

For this reason (the abyss never opens at their feet), they do not require a theology of crisis. They do not ask for a faith to support them in some disaster. They detest extremes. They do not care to see or hear of others exploring the heights and depths which they themselves have never encountered. They ask that their fellows should live with them on their own cozy level of easy laughter and easy tears. The temptation that assails them is this: that they should pervert the Christian message into a sentimental exhortation to all men to inhabit their own congenial sphere of shallow good-fellowship in which there are no clashing opposites, no colliding issues, no black and no white. Their temptation is to pervert the Christian message into an invitation to drop all differences, abandon all principles, lay aside all dogma and rules, and be friendly, tolerant, easy-going, with the same ready smile for everybody.

The tragedy of this attitude is that it corrupts all it touches, and cheapens so much that is precious. Charity is turned into sentimentality, and tolerance into unprincipled anarchy. The emotions are a great quicksand: they can swallow up spirituality, rational doctrine, moral principles. It is one of the most lamentable weaknesses of our age that men and women, professing Christians, allow their own souls, their own intellects, their own wills to be gobbled up by their ravenous emotions. These words are not at all too strong; for they draw attention to a process of self-deception which corrodes integrity and, in the end, annihilates personal identity. This is how the process works. "God is love," they say. "He wants us all to live in fellowship and harmony. The enemies of that fellowship and harmony are those awful Christians who create divisions by pressing extremes, such as insisting upon doctrines about the supernatural, calling for definitions, and talking about authority. The very same people," they say, "create bad relations between Churchmen and outsiders by their bigoted claims. Christianity really means living in love with all men—those inside the Church as well as those outside it. And we must not do anything or say anything to keep the outsiders out—we must

61

keep quiet about miracles and the Trinity and anything offensive to 'modern thought'; we must not have anything to do with fasts and feasts and observances that make Church people look *different*. We must not press moral issues, such as divorce and remarriage, which will cause trouble." And so on—and all, mind you, in the name of "charity"—all in the name of tolerance, good fellowship, the "family spirit."

By evading disciplines which would make us appear "different," we destroy our spiritual integrity. By evading issues which would reveal the Christian faith as something "different," we destroy our intellectual integrity. By evading principles which would show the Christian life to be something "different," we destroy our moral integrity. If, by these evasions, we imagine that we are doing something in the interest of Christian charity, we fool ourselves mightily. Actually we are only satisfying our easy-going emotions, for resting by the gentle waters of cozy tranquillity and in the warm sun of popularity, we have devoured our souls, our intellect, our wills.

That is, of course, an extreme example of how self-deception can work its havoc; but like all the lop-sided religious emphases so far mentioned, self-deception is more prevalent in diluted form than in concentrated form. Perhaps we have had a dose of it ourselves. Was there, for instance, an occasion when we said "Yes" to a thoroughly pagan proposition about faith or morals only because we didn't want the bother of arguing, having a scene, and perhaps losing a friendly acquaintance? It was our charity, we said. But was it? Could it have been only a sentimental self-indulgence?

Was there not another occasion when we smiled and nodded as Mr. Jones made a statement about the Church which, we well knew, totally under-estimated its status, its authority, and its claim? After all, Mr. Jones is our superior, so it was our duty to keep quiet. That was the virtue of obedi-ence in action, we said. Moreover, Mr. Jones is officially a fellow Christian, and outsiders ought not to see us Christians disagreeing among our-selves, we said. That was the virtue of loyalty with more than a dash of charity and humility. Blessed are the peacemakers, we said.

But was it really obedience, loyalty, charity, which plastered a smile on our face while the Church was depreciated from within? A depreci-ation of our Mother, the Body of Christ and the fellowship of saints and martyrs, some of whom thought it better to die rather than to drop a pinch of incense and mutter a meaningless formula?

Obedience, loyalty, and charity? Or was it treachery and betrayal—a mean evasion of those hard realities which hammer against the cushioned smugness of the sentimental self?

It is thus that emotionalism eats into the spiritual, the rational, and the moral content of the faith. Let us take another example. A vital element. of the spiritual life (like penance or fasting), a fundamental doctrine of the Church's creeds (like her teaching on the Trinity), or an unfashionable article in the Church's moral code (like the veto on remarriage after divorce)—one of these is attacked or depreciated or notably ignored, explicitly or implicitly, in statements made in our presence or in actions impinging upon our personal lives. Whichever one it is, for the sake of an easy-going sentimental coziness, we let it go. We do not counter, contradict, or protest. We fit in. Implicitly we betray the faith we profess; by the act of betrayal we make another installment on the purchase of unruffled likeability. No raised eyebrows, no bristling, no edginess—nothing like that with us. We're not going to be known as cranks or difficult people. We're buying a much better name ("He's a good sort. Interested in the Church—but not narrow or anything like that. He can get along with everyone.") and we're buying it by regular payments in the form of smooth little treacheries. God forgive us!

Of the five ways in which we can offer to God a unrecognizable mutilated humanity, the last one is by putting only the body at His disposal— by presenting it there in His Church, at His altar, bereft of intellect or will, a useless carcass. The possibility of having a religious life which involves the body exclusively or predominantly is perhaps less likely today, and it may not be, in its crudest form, much of a temptation at all; nevertheless we must see how the temptation operates, for we have met it—at least in its subtler shapes.

In the first place, this temptation would lead us to a religion of mere outward show—mere physical activity. It happens when the religious life consists of allowing the body to attend Church regularly and perhaps even to take part in Church activities while inwardly the soul and the intellect are entirely dormant and the will makes no movement towards self-surrender. No doubt this temptation was a bigger danger last century than it is now: in the last century certain social motives helped to draw people to Church, and no doubt many people went through the motions without allowing what they did or said or heard to have the slightest effect upon their souls, their brains, or their wills. Now that the cruder ulterior motives for attending Church and concerning oneself with Church life are more or less non-existe᾽ there is no point in highlighting the familiar car᾽ᵃ⁻ ture of the Victorian hypocrite who managedᵗᵒ combine dutifulness in Church observance with brutal exploitation of the poor and a total blindness to spiritual and doctrinal matters.

The other extreme of an exclusively physical religious life is even more unfashionable in the twentieth century; namely, an ostentatious practice of austerities and ascetic self-disciplines which are undertaken for vanity and display rather than out of a true hunger for the spiritual life. Ours is not a civilization in which men try to advertise themselves by wearing a hair shirt or tramping to sacred shrines with nails in their shoes. To gain notoriety these days, it is easier (and much more pleasant) to have five wives in rapid succession than to wall up oneself in an anchorite's cell.

Though neither of these two dangers assails us in an acute or extreme form, we can nevertheless learn something of the less sensational, the less crude temptations which operate insidiously in our own lives. We are all tempted at some time to do something in the way of religious duties merely for the sake of appearances, merely so that we shall be *known* to have done it. Anything done for the sake of appearances demands visible movements of the body, for it is only in the body's movements that others see or hear us—and speech of the tongue is such a movement; it is only the movements of our body which can provide others with something to talk about, something to admire. If we fulfill any religious duty—whether it be going to Confession, attending a weekday celebration of the Eucharist, or collecting rummage, merely so that we shall be *seen* in that duty and *known* to have performed it, we have tried to put a soul-less, thought-less, purpose-less, and feeling-less body into the hands of Almighty God. He asked for a man—or a woman, but we have responded by dumping a carcass at His feet.

Likewise, if we observe certain articles in the Church's moral code with the single motive of being *seen* and *known* to have observed them, and with no thought of obedience, once more we act in the interests of outward appearances only. Whenever, whether for a half hour or for a few moments, our thoughts and purposes and aspirations are withdrawn from the company of our bodies as they kneel or sit in church, to roam far away from anything that properly appertains to worship, we are again trying to give to the Creator of heaven and earth a useless fragment of what it is our duty and privilege to offer inviolate; we are trying to buy God with the mere husk of our humanity.

A religion of only outward motions, of only visible and audible activities, is nothing but a religion of the body. Those of us who enjoy the full inheritance of the Catholic tradition, those of us whose bodies yield so easily to Catholic practice, need especially to take note of this. We speak of offering ourselves, our souls and bodies, to be a reasonable, holy, and living sacrifice to Almighty God. After such fine words, dare we try to trick God with an empty shell?

The gist of this chapter has been that our religious life must involve the offering to God of our full humanity. The Catholic Faith, with its emphatic insistence upon all the rich implications of the Doctrine of the Incarnation, cannot in any way accommodate the notion of a spiritual culture *in vacuo*, in a vacuum. Something more is required of us than the nurturing of our souls: we are asked to put all our human faculties at God's disposal; we are required to put our whole lives under His direction. The case implicitly argued here is this: if our lives are meant to constitute a complete and balanced offering to God, at the center of those lives must be specifically religious practices which themselves involve the whole man. Unless we are bringing our full humanity to the altar, unless we are waiting upon God with all our faculties, we cannot expect our religious practices and observances to bear fruit in every department of our daily lives. Religious practices which involve only fragments of our human endowment will never bring the grace of God to bear full force upon our lives and personalities. Our religious life must involve not only the cultivation of the soul, but also the application of the intellect, the training of the will, the discipline of the emotions, and the homage of the body. Only thus will our religious practices become the vehicle of a supernatural grace that reaches every little corner of our lives.

4

WAITING UPON GOD

THE divine and the human, the eternal and the temporal meet at every stage in the fully Christian pilgrimage. The aim of the Christian is so to surrender his will to God that his human faculties—his hands, his senses, his brain—operate always in accordance with God's purposes. The aim presupposes that God's purposes (and they are always good purposes) are operative within history, within our world, and that free agents like ourselves can submit to them or resist them. It presupposes that every man has the capacity to become acquainted with God's will for him and to adjust himself to it. This is what lends to the Christian life its dignity, its depth, its peace, and its dread. This is what makes the Christian conception of man's earthly life so different from that of the skeptic. For example, right now, as you read these words, you are alive to a dimension of being which the skeptic, because he is a skeptic, cannot acknowledge. You, the Christian, can at this very moment, if you wish, close this book and bend all your inner faculties to the realization of that dimension. Make no mistake about it: it is your contact with that dimension and your entries into the fuller awareness of that dimension which fundamentally differentiate you from the unbeliever. All else you share with him. Like him, you have, at this moment, physical contact with your earthly environment—a chair and its comfort, a furnace and its warmth (or an air-conditioner and its coolness), a reading lamp and its brightness. Like him, you have memories which reach back through twenty, thirty, forty years of earthly experience, and hopes which reach forward into the future. Like him, a compound of brains and emotions and appetites, you are moving forward through time—from birth to death, alternately contacting, and withdrawing from, objects and creatures of a finite world. But unlike him, unlike the unbeliever, you are alert to the voice, the commands, the impulses which issue from another world: if in any sense you are a practicing Christian you are daily alert to what comes into your world from outside its boundaries. You, the Christian, go through life that way: your ears are cocked, your eyebrows are raised, and your head is turned as you wait, listen, and search for the words and movements of God. That is what distinguishes your inner life from that of the unbe-

71

lievers—that established practice (now rooted in you by habit and discipline) of being in contact with God—that expectancy of yours—that sharpened sensitivity which registers whenever God moves you or speaks to you.

As you read these words, you may say to yourself, "No, I'm not in the least like that—perhaps I ought to be, but I'm not." You exaggerate, for *not in the least* is too strong a phrase, much too sweeping. It is the writer's duty to contradict you. You are certainly, most certainly, in some measure "like that"—awaiting word from God, or you wouldn't be reading this book. You wouldn't be bothering at all about a Lenten book, if it were not that by Christian training and habit you are already established in the way of looking beyond the world for the voice of God. What else are you hoping for when you pick up a religious book, if not that something of a message from God may somehow have gotten into it; that God may have contrived to insert there something you need to know; that God may have managed to impart some truth there—perhaps with the help of the writer's perceptiveness, or perhaps despite the writer's obtuseness?

That is what you expect, that is what you are seeking, when you read your Bible, when you pray, when you go to Church, listen to a sermon, read a religious book or a religious article—you are expecting word from beyond the world about you.

It is true, of course, that we don't listen well enough, that we are not always alert, that we are often only half awake spiritually, and that when the word is quietly spoken we fail to notice it or don't try to understand it because of our spiritual selfishness and inertia. It may also be true that our training has advanced but little beyond the most elementary stage, but *it has begun*—indeed it has, for otherwise we should not be meeting like this, you and I together, listening for word from beyond the world; you with the book, I with the pen, each of us—waiting.

Now do you think that an extravagant claim is being made for the priest in the pulpit, or for the writer in his book, when it is said that God may speak to you through their words? The claim does not, by any means, exalt the priest or the writer as individuals; rather it submerges them. What is maintained is this: if there is any thing true and significant in their utterance, it has been put there by God: it is God's revelation to them, not their own discovery; it is God's work, not theirs; they are only His instruments, and God has been using them. That is exactly in line with the Church's

Doctrine of Grace and her teaching about the Holy Spirit. When we do good, it is the work of grace in us; it is the fruit of our submission to the will of God. When we do ill, it is the work of evil in us; it is the fruit of our resistance to the promptings of the Holy Spirit. In the same way, when we speak or write truly of God, when our utterance, however halting and incomplete, reveals something of His nature, something of His purpose and His message for men, that too is the work of grace in us; it is the fruit of our submission to the guidance of the Holy Spirit. When we speak inadequately, or misleadingly, or even falsely, of God and His ways, it is the work of our very own assertive wills, perverted by selfishness, and of our obstinate minds, dulled by pride and blinded by worldliness. The enlightening word of truth, in a sermon or a book, is the work of God. The ineffective, unworthy, unrevealing utterance is the contribution of the speaker or writer.

There is nothing new or original in this idea: it is, from the aesthetic point of view, merely the age-old "doctrine of the muse" brought up to date. Every good writer knows that the utterances which are *given* to him express the truest and surest insights and that it is compelling, urgent, and necessary for him to convey that vision; but all that he frantically slaps together by straining his brain, by toilsome artifice, by slavishly driving his pen by the whip of his will, is so truly his *own* work that it is worthless.

However abused or misused it may be, this is God's world; He made it, and, whether we see it now or later—or never, He runs it. There has been no divine abdication. We must expect to see His hand at work in some of the things that happen in the world. Let us not therefore imagine that we can wait upon the word of God only by withdrawing ourselves from all that has material existence. No doubt a temporary withdrawal from the world of sense and matter can be a fruitful spiritual discipline; no doubt God speaks in the great spiritual silences into which mystics have plunged by their cumulative negations; but God also speaks through the words of a friend, a sermon in the pulpit, a voice on the TV, a page of a book. Indeed, the echo of God's voice can be caught in the utterances of men who claim not to know Him, even of men who would stoutly deny Him. The movement of His hand can be detected, now here, now there, in the acts of men and in the events that overtake them. It is a blind man indeed who cannot see the Devil at work in the world today; it is an unbelieving man who cannot see God at work there. Failure to detect the Devil's machinations around us is due to our obtuseness; failure to detect God's care and guidance about us is due to a deficiency of faith.

In the Church, as once in the flesh, our Lord is in the world, and the world knows Him not. We who are in the Church, companying with our Lord, would indeed be guilty of infidelity if we did not expect God's care to be about us, if we did not daily open ourselves to His word. There is nothing very mystical about our openness to God's word. You and I are not monks and nuns, and our daily program does not include long periods of silence and solitude and the practice of advanced spiritual exercises and various methods of contemplation. On the contrary, if we try so much as to extend our Lenten allocation of time for prayer and meditation, we find that our immediate environment rises in noisy opposition. Is there anything, anything at all, which does not militate against our fitful attempts to bring the way of the cloister into our home? Go down on your knees in the bedroom or the kitchen for an extra session with God, fully determined to allow patience to ripen into silence, silence into utter receptiveness, and what happens? The telephone rings, or a neighbor drops in, or the baby starts to cry. Margaret decides to practice her piano lesson, and little Johnny rehearses his newly-achieved leap from the newel post. A plane roars overhead, across the street a truck warms up, and a TV show turned up by those incorrigible low-brows next door seems to flood the whole house. It isn't always the same set of impediments, of course, for there is an inexhaustible supply of them in endless variety. That's the cunning of it. You can't defend yourself adequately in advance. Not until you make a determined effort to extend your prayer life do you fully realize how many type-writers, trombones, loud-speakers, clocks, bells, and buses there are in the world. Not until then do you glimpse the monstrous mass of ingenious devices that militate against utter quiet: vacuum cleaners, trains, drills, bull-dozers, hucksters, ambulances, and—for some people—noises less fiendish, but not less distracting, produced by children; children laughing, screaming, singing, banging spoons, bursting paper bags, blowing whistles, and swinging rattles.

Well, now, we must be sensible. That's the world God has put us in, and He knows how noisy it is. We can't begin to behave as though it were a region of rarefied spiritual silence if it is chock full of thumps and shrieks and clatters. You can't lead the life of a contemplative nun with infant twins yowling in their pen, with Grandmother yakking in the kitchen, and with a husband due home from the office at 5:30.

We must remember, however, that just as our Lord has led us through death, so has He led us through life—through this life. He was God Incarnate, God in flesh, God in a real, solidly human home, with a pre-electric saw buzzing in the background. Our Lord, we have said, plunged down to the very depths of creation, took His own divinity to that lowly level where man eats and drinks the fruits of the earth. God is not beaten by twentieth-century factory whistles, passing trains, or a half-deaf neighbor's addiction to TV westerns. If, deep in your will, there is the desire that God should be with you, He will be there— he will break through any sound barrier, however hideous.

What, then, is this alertness, the openness, this watchfulness, with which we daily wait upon God? It is a single-hearted conviction that we ourselves and all things terrestrial stand at all times under God. It is the quiet assurance that He has his good purposes for us and for all things terrestrial that stand under Him. It is the unfretting acceptance of what His providence and our sense of duty lay upon us. It is the unshakable faith that through all things He *cares,* and that whenever needful He will speak. Patience, acceptance, quiet—inner qualities, maintained even when noise and tumult are about us—they are the good soil in which the seed of His word can be fruitfully sown.

Just how will God's word reach you? Sometimes, perhaps, through a notion or a phrase suddenly and directly planted in your mind. More often through one of those numerous human means which God has used since the Incarnation made humanity the vehicle of the divine: through the words of a friend, through an odd sentence in a book or a sermon, through a verse from the Bible pondered in that ten minutes snatched for meditation, through the words of a hymn or a psalm suddenly seen in a fresh light.

But we *must* look and listen—we must expect God to speak, we must treat this world in its relation to another—dependent upon another. That is a precondition of any kind of contact with God. If we treat our world as the only thing there is or ever will be, by binding ourselves implicitly to its material values, by lawlessly feeding our appetites with what it offers the senses, and by acting as though we had no responsibilities beyond it, indeed the word of God will never be heard—it will never reach us, because a prior and absolute attachment to this world is a sound-proof wall between God and ourselves.

Getting in touch with God is not a matter of desperately straining to push over some barrier, to penetrate some deep darkness; it is not a case of setting out to struggle through a tangled, little-trodden terrain to a far-off, withdrawn deity: God has not hedged Himself about with impenetrable buffer states. (Metaphors which stress the heroic toil of the Christian pilgrimage are necessary in certain contexts, but they can be dangerously misleading at times.) In the business of opening ourselves to God, the activity is not ours but His; the search is not ours but His. This is one reason we must not fret if our individual circumstances seem to restrict our opportunities for reflection and meditation. (With many of us such opportunities are much greater than we pretend: we are not all bound by a ceaseless round of duties to young children, sick dependents, and failing grandparents.) Provided we make use of the opportunities offered to us, God will get through to us. We are not engaged in a great exploration, a great seeking for God: He is seeking us, and He will find us, if only we take the trouble to put ourselves in His way.

That is the important thing. We have to put ourselves in God's way. He is speaking all the time, but we have to go within hearing distance and listen for whatever is meant for us personally. He is speaking all the time—now, in the Bible on the bookshelf behind you: you may take it down at any moment and listen for something particularly addressed to you. He is speaking now, as you sit at home and read. He is speaking through the psalms and lessons of the Daily Offices in your parish church; He spoke there this morning, and perhaps more than once, through the Epistle and Gospel for the day. He speaks through your parish priest in the confessional, when he gives you absolution, when he lays a penance upon you, when he gives you spiritual direction. He speaks through the words of all who write authoritatively, to give testimony or counsel on living the Christian life. Indeed, He speaks through all religious books whose message is in accord with the Church's teaching. Of course, if you don't take the trouble to go where His voice can be heard, you will certainly not hear Him.

No message in the twentieth century of Christendom is more urgent than this: God *is busy* among us *all the time*. He does not lounge around and hope that someone or other, two or three or more if possible, will bestir themselves today in His service so that the day will not be completely lost; He does not sit upon His throne and dream of a time when all men will discover Him and something will be done in a really big way. Quite to the contrary, God is active among us daily; and either we are involved in His activity, or we are resisting Him; we are either a help or a hindrance.

God is especially active in and through His Church. At altars He daily offers His Flesh and Blood for the building up of men in His Divine Body. We must not get into the habit of saying, "Tomorrow I will do something special for God. I will get up and go to Church early." We must not say that, nor must we picture God as a chronic invalid—one for whom our early morning visit has the refreshing sparkle of the unexpected guest or the unsolicited dish of ice cream brought to the sick room. No, we can't get up before God is stirring. And when we "serve Him," it isn't like taking flowers to a patient in the hospital. It is more like leaping on a passing bus. So we must say, "God gives Himself daily at the altar. God speaks daily from the sanctuary. Tomorrow, for once, I'll not be among the missing: I'll be there, in His Church, to receive and to hear."

Nothing more positive is demanded of us than that we should be there, where God is, to see what He is doing, to hear what He is saying—now, today. If only we could get it into our heads that when God comes into our midst, as He comes daily in our parish churches, the odd, the remarkable, the astonishing thing is that there should be Christians within reach who are *not* there! That Christians are missing is an extraordinary fact that requires explanation or excuse. Here is God, giving Himself in the Blessed Sacrament, performing His tireless work, giving, stirring, nurturing, speaking—and we are not there. We are missing; but when we do bestir ourselves and come to the altar, we have the effrontery (or is it irony, or our idea of humor?) to flatter ourselves that we are *doing* something! And to make it worse, we tell ourselves that we are doing something for God!

If we put ourselves in the way of God, and put ourselves there on our knees, He will speak to us, lift us up, and take us along with Him. It is not that He is accessible and we must approach Him, but rather that He is approaching and we must be accessible. It is not that He is silent and we must stir Him by our prayers and utterances, but rather that He is speaking and we must stop what we are doing in order to hear Him. It is not that He is on a holiday—away from the world of men—and we must struggle to keep His work going in His absence, but rather that He is always wrestling with the world's agonies and its corruptions (what does the Incarnation mean, if not that?), that He is daily sweeping into the hearts of men with a cleansing wind and a purging fire (for wherever the conscience stirs, is not the hand of God at work?), that He is hourly plunging into the depths of the human, into the heart of the natural, simply to salvage the souls of men. All of that is always going on—nothing less than the labor of seeking and saving eternally. Either we are involved in it, with God; or we are outside it, and against Him.

Having now defined generally the Christian's duty to put himself at the disposal of God, in openness and availability to Him, let us see, with some system, what all this involves.

We wait upon God at His altar

This first: in the Church's worship generally, and in the Eucharist in particular, we present ourselves under the stupendous claim to be very members of Christ's Body, and, fulfilling His command, partake of that Food which nourishes us as such.

Here, as the Church pleads before God the one perfect sacrifice of humanity divinized and offered up to Him, heaven and earth, the temporal and the eternal, meet more surely and more conclusively than at any other point in time and space. As we offer ourselves under cover of our Lord's wholly acceptable self-oblation, the divine goes past lips and teeth and tongue, through throat and gullet to the stomach and intestines, to the very center of our physical humanity. This great act is a guarantee of the validity and the value of our humanity—a humanity moulded of solid dust and fiber and enlivened by breath and fire. This great act involves us wholly in membership of that Body which is His on earth, it involves us wholly in what He wills and performs here on earth—wholly, from the tip of the toenail to the crown of the head, from the level at which we sniff with delight a turkey roasting in the oven or the scent of a good cigar, to the level at which we dissect the atom, ponder the mystery of being, or give of our substance and our sympathy to the sick and the suffering.

In the Eucharist our whole humanity waits upon God; in it our whole humanity is fed by God. There is the offering of our full humanity, the cleansing of it, the appropriation of it. It is taken over by God as a mother takes over an adopted child: it is fed at God's table and assumed into His family, its life and, its eternalness. That is what happens. We fall in line to offer ourselves, and God appropriates us. Of course it may be that afterwards, before we have reached our car or the sidewalk, we have snatched ourselves back from God and reasserted a private ownership of ourselves. It may be that, before the end of day, we have paid a subscription, or given active support, to the great twentieth-century movement for Human Self-Determination, the movement which campaigns against God's oppressive and tyrannical right to requisition human beings: it all depends on how turbulent, how rebellious, how unregenerate our ego is. For some of us, who cherish our assertive little selves like so many little god almighties, self-offering is an almost intolerable torment. Let us face the facts: we are dealing with an ever-encroaching, always omnicompetent God; and whenever we go to Church and offer ourselves, we voluntarily put ourselves within reach of His compulsory purchase order. In every communion God requisitions a human soul.

We wait upon God in prayer and meditation

The practice of prayer and meditation is one sure safeguard against the danger mentioned above —the danger that between our communions we shall repossess ourselves, try to snatch our humanities back from the hand of God. In our communions God claims and sanctifies our offered humanity, but, after we have turned our back on His altar and returned to the world of daily affairs, nothing is easier than virtually annulling our offering and denying the continuing validity of God's claim. Nothing is easier and nothing more natural by virtue of the very quality of our world itself, for it is not an *offering* world—and that is what distinguishes it from the Church. The Church is a sphere of offering—of giving and not keeping; the world is a sphere of getting and having.

It is therefore necessary to turn from this world, to focus the mind and heart and will upon God who alone can change getting and having into giving and not keeping. To turn in openness and in renewed self-offering is to turn to God and hear what He has to say. Prayer and meditation are together processes of offering and listening: both are means by which we wait upon God.

The praise and gratitude which we offer God are due Him for being what He is, and for having done what He has done. We offer ourselves in penitence and self-giving; we plead for mercy for all that we have wilfully done to separate ourselves from Him, for weakening or destroying His possession of our humanity; and once more, by conscious direction of the will, we put ourselves wholly and forgivenly at His disposal. We offer the needs of the whole world—the sufferings of afflicted men and women, the writhings and self-torture of rebellious men and women, the claims, the hunger, and the dissatisfactions of spiritually-deprived men and women. That sums up the content of Christian prayer—it is all offering and waiting.

And meditation is all listening and waiting. We prepare ourselves by silence, by abstracting ourselves from our familiar world of getting and having and entering the world of offering. We ask God, not for this or that favor (for ourselves or for anyone), but simply to speak to us. We read a short passage from the Bible, and we dwell on especially chosen and significant phrases. We do not make a great mental effort to fit their messages into a favorite thought-pattern of our own devising; rather, we open ourselves to what God has to say to us through them. We think, not constructively, but receptively. It is the kind of thinking which a writer is always having to do, but it is done in meditation—within the discipline of conscious commitment to God, and under cover of an invocation to the Holy Spirit.

Our regular daily periods of private prayer and meditation sustain us in self-offering from one communion to the next. Between our periods of private prayer, our practice should be to turn our thoughts momentarily to God as frequently as our occupations allow. All those who have advanced far in the spiritual life urge us to cultivate this habit of committing ourselves at frequent intervals with a very brief prayer of, say, only one or two sentences. It may take the form of a simple act of praise, thanks, faith, hope, love, penitence, or self-surrender; or it may consist of a text remembered purposefully from our last meditation. If our communions are our spiritual feasts, and our periods of private prayer and meditation are our daily spiritual meals, the intermittent acts of commitment may be likened to the snacks in between. This metaphor, however, might offend the abstemious.

We wait upon God in study

A less important way of exercising and deepening our openness to God is by the study of religious books. It is far less important than sacrament, prayer, and meditation (which involves study of the Bible, of course), but still it is important—important for most people and very important for many; it is especially important for those who read habitually, and still more important for those who read a great deal. As Christians, we are necessarily all worshippers, all pray-ers, but how many of us are, or ought to be, readers? How many of us ought be be reading religious books fairly often, or more often than we do?

All Christians who habitually read in order to gain information, or to be entertained in some way, ought to be prepared to read also in order to learn more about God and His Church. And that means all who peruse the daily newspapers beyond pictures and headlines, all who use public libraries, all who take magazines. Should not the housewife who regularly picks up a copy of *Woman's Day* in the A & P, or the corporation executive who reads *Fortune* in bed, or the widow who is on the library's mystery-book waiting list—should not they read also about God, His ways, His Church? The truth is that the secular press, as a whole, presents us with a picture of life from which God is totally absent: its tone, its values, its judgments are all rooted and grounded in this world. In popular journalism, and in popular literature generally, there is a strong current of unregenerate worldliness in which we, our brains and our emotions, will drift, unless we firmly hold to our course.

Precisely because our Lord sanctified, perfected,

and offered up a full humanity, we must offer up a full humanity too, and that means not just the soul and the will but also the intellect. By the very nature of our civilization, the printed word enormously influences the character of our personalities, and we cannot regard ourselves as even *trying* to be at God's disposal unless we allow our brains access to material which conveys or interprets God's truth.

Two points need to be mentioned here. In the first place, our civilization is a highly intellectualized one. That does not mean that we have a high level of intellectual achievement; rather it means that we have an unprecedented quantity of intellectual activity.. The quality of that activity is another matter. Within the Church a considerable body of thinkers is producing a great number of books: insofar as they deal with technical matters—biblical criticism, history, religious philosophy, liturgics, and the like, they have no great significance for the non-specialist; but there are plenty of books which expound the faith, teach what the Church is, what her message means, and what the Christian life really is, and they are meat and drink for minds starved or impoverished by the worldly diet of popular journalism. God will speak to us through them; He is already speaking in them. But if we never open one of them, we may deprive ourselves of an opportunity to hear the voice of God.

The other point is this: by what is perhaps a peculiar irony, the twentieth-century's return to the Faith has been led by our intellectuals. There is no predominantly proletarian return to God, but we can detect among intellectuals, writers, and artists, and the cultured classes generally, a body of Christian opinion large and strong enough to be called a "movement." It is mostly through books, at the present, that the influence of the movement can be exerted upon a wider public. Church men and women need to be acquainted with some of that wealth of contemporary literature which has power to drive some belief into the thoughtful outsider.

The most compelling reason for reading religious books is that God speaks through them. No Christian who has taken time to read religious books can deny that time after time a sentence has leaped out at him from the middle of a page to answer the gravest, the deepest need of the moment. Let me tell you how it works. A sentence from perhaps a rather long book, or a single argument from a rather long chapter, hits us in the face: it seems to have been meant for us and us alone. It is the one piece of spiritual advice or instruction pre-eminently needed at the moment. It stays with us for a week, or a month, and lights up a hitherto dark situation or stills a hitherto anguished cry of rebellion. God has done that for us. He has chosen to speak to us in precisely that way. Every year thousands of new religious books testify to His choice. We shall do well not to turn away from Him here—or anywhere.

We wait upon God in obedience

So far we have spoken of the ways in which we must put ourselves at God's disposal in matters which might be called "religious"—that is, in religious practices and religious study, but now we must speak of an availability to God in matters which do not readily present themselves to us as part of our specifically "religious" life.

To start with, we must put ourselves at God's disposal by developing a disciplined sensitiveness to the work of His hand in our midst. We must re-learn the awareness of Divine Providence which our age seems to have lost. In other words, we must trust. But that does not mean cultivating a vague feeling in the back of the mind that every cloud has a silver lining and that if winter comes spring cannot be far behind. Trust is not the same thing as optimism; nor is trust the same thing as hope. Trust is a *present* thing, and it attaches itself to *particular* situations. To trust in God is to have the assurance that God has a role for us in a given situation, and that does not necessarily mean an easy or a comfortable role. To trust is to have the assurance that God *can* be served in a particular situation, and that He will, if we are attentive, show us the appointed way of our service.

This lesson urgently needs to be impressed on our twentieth-century minds: we are always running away from difficult situations, avoiding things; we are always saying, "If only such-and-such had been different, I could have done this or that. As it is I can do nothing." "If only my boss were a man of understanding . . ." "If only Mrs. Green weren't president of the guild . . ." "If only Father Brown knew how to handle people . . ." "If only the Bishop had some understanding of the Faith of the Church . . . " "*If only*," we say, and then shrug our shoulders. Our attitude implies— *this is a bad situation; God can't possibly expect me to do anything about it.* We have every right to make the first statement (this is a bad situation), but we have no right whatsoever to make the second one (God can't expect me to do anything about it). The first statement may represent a proper exercise of balanced human reason, but the second statement is a denial of the Christian duty of trust. Goodness knows there are plenty of bad situations in the world, and we are in them most of the time—it is that kind of a world, but there is *never* a situation in which we cannot in some way serve God.

We cannot allow ourselves to have an attitude which says that a situation is "impossible" or "hopeless." True, there are plenty of bad situations, but—for the Christian—there are no impossible ones, no hopeless ones. (The only hopeless situation is that of the damned.) "This is a bad situation," we may say. "It has been produced by wholesale disobedience to the will of God. What does God want *me* to do about it? If I can't do anything about it, why is God keeping me here? That I am here means that there *is* something I can do!" That is trust. In that way we lay ourselves open to the guidance of God; in that way we make ourselves available; in that way we offer ourselves for use—in the situation in which God has seen fit to place us.

There is nothing negative about it at all, nor is there any hint of inertia or resignation. God does not always tell us to sit quietly and suffer in silence. Sometimes He tells us to rebuke the wrong-doer. God's servants are by no means expected meekly to keep their mouths shut while the Devil's fellow-travellers vote all his nominees into office or see that they get the key positions; but (and it is a strong but) we have to be careful, scrupulously careful, that when we act in the name of God we are not furtively pleasing ourselves. It is so easy to turn our support of a cause, especially of an unpopular one, into nothing more than mere self-assertion. When we see that we are really "in doubt" in a difficult situation, in a bad situation, in a devil-planned situation, we may be tempted to do nothing at all, on the grounds that outraged reason and conscience proclaim the situation impossible, or we may be tempted to explode in violent indignation and fierce action which, though masquerading as the earthly fruits of divine displeasure, are actually orgies of egotistical self-indulgence. The only safeguard against these pernicious temptations is a continuous and conscious openness to God's guidance, stimulated and disciplined by regular prayer and meditation, and supported, where available, by spiritual direction. "Yea, hath *God* said"?

The truth is that in such situations we ought to be much more on the watch for God's intervention. Our watchfulness, if undisciplined and carried to a fantastic extreme, can of course produce dangerous states of mind and highly irrational behavior, but the greater danger is our particular age in history is to undervalue or ignore Divine Providence. If that is so, there is all the greater need to point out that our Christian teaching about the nature of God, His relationship to the world, and the function of human prayer, necessarily presupposes that God is active in our midst, that He does indeed guide those who freely put themselves at His disposal. Just as in a personal dilemma he may speak to us through a sermon or a book, so in the same way in some social tangle over policy or relationships He may act in the sudden removal of a person or an obstacle, or in the sudden addition of a new person, a new issue, a new possibility. Thus we have to learn adaptability—adaptability to God, for that is the bedrock of practical obedience. If we do not, through self-discipline, learn adaptability to God, we shall most certainly, through default, acquire adaptability to the world, and so destroy our trust in God.*

Practical obedience, by which we strive daily to serve God in all the affairs of life, is the fruit of a quiet, inner waiting upon His word. Gradually,

*The practical implications of Christian teaching about personal obedience are explored at some length in the author's *The Will and the Way* (The Macmillan Co.).

by the grace of God, we must silence the nagging voice of self-will which is accustomed to raise itself as the guide of our behavior on any and every occasion. Gradually, and by the same grace, we must learn to be, without fuss and to-do, inwardly, reflectively open to God. Where, for any length of time, there has been a swelling egotism, inserting itself into every situation with a demand for attention and satisfaction, it may be silenced by that still, calm blend of outward-looking assurance and expectancy which we call trust: trust in God. He is *always willing* a course of action for us; and always it is our business to find out what it is—for today, tomorrow, and the day after. The assurance that God is always willing a course of action for us is a fruit of faith; that it is our business to find out exactly what He is willing is the fact of freedom.

We find out by listening.

We wait upon God in charity

Perhaps the most difficult lesson of all to learn is that by opening ourselves to God we look for Him in others: it means seeing our Lord in other men and women, and seeing other men and women in Him. Obedience is the art of seeing ourselves in particular, and our world generally, under *God*, and acting accordingly. Charity is the act of seeing our fellow creatures *under God*—and acting accordingly. We wait upon God in obedience when we see His hand reaching into our little world, restraining us here, impelling us there, training this man's patience to a fruitful joy, and bringing that man's vanity to a corrective discipline. We wait upon God in obedience when we see this and submit ourselves prayerfully, yieldingly, in cooperation. We wait upon God in charity when we see the suffering of our Lord in the face of the contorted paralytic or in the wasted body of a refugee, or when we see the innocence of our Lord in the eyes of a guileless child. We wait upon God in charity when we see this and give freely and prayerfully of the strength, the sympathy, the comfort so freely given to us.

Let us suppose that we have just begun to learn this lesson, you and I, that we have gotten so far that we cannot see affliction without saying a silent prayer: the bed-ridden, the cripple, the blind, the maimed, the mentally-ill, the neurotic— when we meet them or when they are brought to our minds, we are stirred to prayers on their behalf and, probably, to those half-ashamed phrases of gratitude for all that we have been given or spared. Suppose, too, that we have gotten so far that we cannot come closely in contact with little children without responding immediately and sensitively to the infinite resources of freshness, joy, and simplicity stored in the heart of the God who created them.

If we have gotten so far—well and good. We have made a little progress—a little, a very little progress, for there is much else to learn. We must not pat ourselves on the back for having acquired a compassion for the miserably afflicted, or found joy in the spectacle of innocence. There is something much harder than that to learn. We have not only to see loveliness in the tragically injured and the beautifully pure, but we must also see in the unattractive, uncongenial, hostile fellow-creature a loveliness—under God and in God we must see him lovely too. Nature may help us to see our Lord's suffering reflected in the ashen pallor and the weariness of an invalid; certainly nature helps us to see the light of our Lord's joy and glory in the smile of a child or in the beauty of a girl, but it takes the grace of God for us to see our Lord's unfailing availability in the man who envies and detests us, who ignores us, who has made us appear ludicrous and contemptible in our feeble attempts to please God. It takes the grace of God for us to see our Lord's unfailing tenderness in the woman who has damaged our reputation with her clever tongue, or who would not hesitate to steal a husband if she had the chance, or who has tried to drag some member of your family through the mud of scandal. It takes God's grace to see God in others.

We are not to be misled by this kind of talk into false sentimentality. Sin is sin, and it has to be hated whether it lurks behind the scowl of an ugly man or behind the smile of a beautiful woman, whether it seats itself in the soul of a harlot or in the soul of a senator. When the Devil gets his claws into the heart of a human creature, whether that person be repulsive or seductive, there must be action, resistance, or constraint. But yet . . . but yet . . . we are all sinners. Perhaps there is not so great a difference between our offenses as we want to picture, and maybe the shelter given to you and me in our upbringing and training makes the influences upon our enemy look, by comparison, like a complete guidebook to damnation. Maybe our early environment, in comparison with his, has been as the cleansed and well-scrubbed kitchen to the reeking sty.

We know, in an ideal way, what our duty is. We have been told often enough. Somehow we must learn to hate the sin and love the sinner—

something that is not always difficult. When the sinner's sins have been directed against others, we find it quite easy to go on loving him; but when the sinner's sins have been directed against ourselves, it's a different matter! The brusque upstanding man, immune in his arrogance, who for ten years has slowly done his calculating best to discredit, defame, and deride us—no, we can never like him, we can never warm up to him, and it would be wrong, we say, to look for any good in his maimed, truncated personality. Can we not, however, learn to wait upon God in that man's presence by recalling that he is God's child too? Can we not remember our common bond—that we are both miserable sinners and equally dependent for all things on God's love and mercy?

What about that keen-eyed, thin-lipped woman who for ten years has skilfully managed to turn every word of ours against us, to humiliate us, to insinuate all sorts of things? No, we can never like her, we can't even smile at her without feeling hypocritical, we don't even want to meet her face to face. Can we learn to wait upon God in her presence by verbally linking ourself with her in our own sinfulness? Can we not say, "God have mercy upon us—both?"

Extreme cases have been cited because it is by

them that wise advice and true teaching are tested. Usually, however, we are not dealing day in and day out with men and women whose souls have been poisoned with envy and hatred; whatever antagonisms we may feel towards others are almost always based upon irritating habits, careless actions, ill-conceived utterances, and temperamental incompatibilities. Often we are dealing with people whom we ourselves have wronged by mis-judging them rather than with people who have gravely and intentionally wronged us. In any case, our duty is the same: we must see them in our Lord, and we must see our Lord in them.

To see them in our Lord is to recognize them as our fellow members in Christ, our brothers and sisters under God: to see them as sinners at our side, dependent along with us upon God's sustaining hand, God's love, God's mercy. To see our Lord in them is to recognize in them whatever virtues and merits they have as the work of God in man. If God has blessed us, He has not withheld his blessing from others.

To see our Lord in them is to look intentionally and purposefully for their virtues, to search for the work of grace in their expressions, their words, their responses, their actions. If we look for it, we shall find it. (No truth is more attested by the saints than that!) If we look for our Lord, we shall find Him, even in the people with the most damaging, the most lowering, the most despicable vices—yes, even in that man or that woman who has detested us for ten long years. Our Lord is there, somewhere; and where He is, it is our duty to wait upon Him—there and then.

We wait upon God in peace

There is no waiting upon God without patience: there must be an inner calm and self-surrender; there must be a deep quietness. If our thoughts and desires roam widely and lawlessly during the Sunday Eucharist, we are not truly waiting upon God at His altar. If our reasoning and aspiring self is not quietly present, but restlessly absent, we are only pretending to wait upon God there—we are only going through the motions of waiting upon Him. If, when we are supposedly involved in prayer and meditation, our mind toys with haphazard ideas and our hopes turn to trivial dreams, we are only *pretending* to wait upon God. Externally we are appearing to wait upon Him, but inwardly we are waiting upon ourselves—and that is a dangerous hypocrisy. Again, if, when we are studying religious books, we are doing so, not because we deeply, unassertively want to know God and His ways, but because we have a climbing, agitated ego inside which wants only to be admired for its knowingness, we are not truly waiting upon God in our reading. Under cover of much pretense, we are waiting upon ourselves.

It is the same when we submit ourselves to Divine Providence by obediently adapting ourselves to God's will—something we must do without fretting for some particular outcome of our endeavors. We cannot submit ourselves obediently to God's will and at the same time push the interests of a nagging and grasping ego under cover of our submission. We dare not verbally profess a surrender to God, and at the same time allow our desires to fasten themselves on some earthly advantage. We must let go, we must be at peace— and to be at peace is to be freed of all those persisting and fretting desires, ambitions, and aspirations which would claim so much of our early future. We must not be forever wanting something. Inner wanting is like the convulsive inner rumbling of an unstable piece of ground: you dare not build on it; you cannot submit yourself to God so long as the rumbling can be detected, the cracking of the surface seen, and the turbulent self is ready to erupt.

Waiting upon God in obedience is the sanctification of the will. Waiting upon God in peace is the sanctification of our desires.

Our will is a vigorous, thrusting thing: it has to be disciplined, directed, contained. Our desires are restless, agitated, surging things: they have to be restrained, calmed, and stilled.

Our selfish desires, our worldly desires feed the assertive self on an indigestible diet of crude longings and vapid imaginings. They stoke up the assertive self's energies. They are always busy, fetching and carrying, foraging and fuelling, to the fattening up of the clamorous and incontinent self. Our selfish desires must be stilled, quieted, and laid to rest.

We wait upon God in tranquillity. It is the only way; for otherwise we wait upon the self.

We wait upon God in Christ

We present ourselves before God only by virtue of our union with Christ; we offer ourselves to God under the cover of our Lord's own offering on the Cross. To offer ourselves in any other way would indicate that we had something of our own to give, or some claim of our own to make. That is one reason why the Eucharist stands at the center of our lives as the most significant, most sublime expression of ourselves in relation to God: because in it we offer that which is not our offering, but our Lord's; because in it we offer ourselves totally, by divesting ourselves of the pretentious claim that we of ourselves have anything to offer.

We come before God claiming nothing for ourselves—nothing except (and it is everything) that we have been embraced and sheltered by the redeeming love of Christ. We wait upon God by plainly asserting that we have no right even to wait upon him—except by virtue of our Lord's suffering on our behalf. We come, yes, but first we divest ourselves of any pretense that we have the right, in our own persons, to be there at all. Thus, at the very center of our religious life, the Eucharist establishes the pattern of all human self-offering.

To wait upon God, to be open to Him, is to be rid of all self-favoritism. We cannot truly offer ourselves to God, to be moulded and used, if we come to Him parading our own estimate of ourselves. If we are living daily in the company of our own cozy estimate of ourselves, cherishing it, trying to impose it upon the world at large—and fretting or sulking when we can't have our way, we cannot openly wait upon God. We are not available so long as we are fondly nursing and feeding that growing estimate of ourselves. It has to be laid aside. It is the deceiving child of deception. Nourished, it will grow into a ravenous monster and devour us. To wait upon God we must keep better company, for we ourselves are nothing —nothing except what God has made us, and we have nothing—nothing except what God has given us, and we can offer nothing—nothing (and it is everything) except the perfect sacrifice of our Lord Himself.

We are nothing: and yet at the same time we *are* something; we are the redeemed children of God, wearing that humanity which He created, which He inhabited, which He renewed. Moreover, we go about our daily living and make the bold claim to be very members of His Body whose offering we dare to offer in the Eucharist. Thus our own claims (the ones we dare not make for ourselves before Him) are trivial, petty, infinitesimal, by comparison with the divinely provided claims which draw us back, week by week, or day by day, to His altar: the claim that we are involved in the great redemptive act by which history was torn open to eternity and humanity was invaded by divinity; the claim that we too are addressed in those astonishing words spoken by God to man: *This is my Body: Take, eat: Do this in remembrance of me.*

THE CHURCH
AND THE WORLD

GOD'S way is not the world's way. The two have been in conflict since the Fall. The world being what it was (and is), the blending of divinity and humanity in our Lord cost the Crucifixion. The blending of humanity and divinity is always costly. If we involve our own humanity in the Divine Action, if we feed our humanity on the Divine Flesh and Blood, a price has to be paid. When the world's way is rejected, the world exacts its pound of flesh: you cannot turn your back upon the world's worldliness and yet preserve the world's respect and benevolence. If you wish to do handsomely in the world, you must wait upon the world, and you cannot wait upon the world when you are waiting upon God. Turn to God, wait upon Him, and He will involve you in the divine plan—the master-scheme of fitting men for heaven. Turn to Him, offer yourself, give Him half a chance, and you will be taken, enrolled, involved in that plan. It is fine and glorious, it is cleansing and humbling; it is deeply rewarding, but it is not—most certainly not—what the world hopes and expects of you. Oh, no, the world expects something a little more sensible, realistic, and "practical" than that. The world is polite, of course; it is very sorry, full of apologies, hates to mention the matter, and so on; but it begs leave to point out that if you *must* go and "sign on" in the service of the Other Firm, a somewhat tangible Firm with rather mysterious and utterly invisible assets, you can't expect to stay on the pay-roll down here.

God's plan is a take-over plan; and the world is in no mood to be taken over. The world values too much what it imagines to be its own autonomy. Pitched between the two great powers bestriding the universe, our little world is shrieking that it wants neutrality and self-determination. The Devil, who has his agents strategically scattered about in the world and in various disguises, has himself prompted the world's call for self-determination, and his own propaganda has encouraged the call, for the Devil knows full well that self-determination means resistance to God and that resistance to God is submission to the Devil. Even the world's government is a puppet one manipulated from hell. It is an occupied world shouting to the liberating God that it will not have its "neutrality" and "independence" tampered with. We Christians are the agents of that liberating God, but those who serve the world so faithfully tell us that we are traitors, escapists, shirkers of our responsibilities, that we are running away from the duties to the world and that we have our heads— our hearts and minds—in the clouds. Up to a point, but only that far, they are right. We are certainly out to betray their puppet government; but those who praise that government in the name of progress, scientific humanism, rationalism, and the like, fail to see that it is a collaborationist government and that the orders come from hell. The government of this world has already secretly sold out to the Devil, and it is only a question of taking all the people with it before it can come out into the open. Time is on the collaborationist's side, but eternity is on the Christian's side: the Christian would sell all to God.

Perhaps the opposition is really beginning, just beginning, to come into the open, for there are indeed signs that such is the case: certainly the thoughtful Christian is never allowed to forget that the world's plan is diametrically opposed to God's plan, and it would be foolish for us to underestimate the cruel tensions of modern life, when it is lived within the Church and in the world as well.

There is no need to exemplify these tensions, for we are all too sadly aware of them. Every year the ethos of the world becomes more and more removed from the ethos of Christendom. And no man can reject the world's ethos without paying a certain price: the world rewards its own faithful soldiers and servants, and in one way or another it punishes its rebels. We Christians are all, of course, its rebels. We reject the central articles of the world's code which makes earthly well-being, physial satisfaction, and material prosperity the prime ends and motives of all "fruitful" and "meritorious" action. We reject also the notion that national, political, social, and personal action always has to be determined by motives of practical expediency (the technical term in politics for selfishness). On the other hand we would substitute certain fixed principles—those of justice, charity, and peace—principles which the politicians talk about but rarely act upon. We abhor the now established practice of using words like justice and peace as mere slogans (deceptive slogans at that), behind which those who hold the reins of power pursue the separate selfish ends of their own nation or their own group. Thus it is that in the first sphere to which our thoughts turn—public action and national politics—we Christians find ourselves at war with the corruptions and deceptions now accepted as the recognized currency of public life.

As Christians we are at war with the philosophy of power or pressure groups, yet our national life is one seething mass of conflicting groups. As Christians we are at war with dishonesty, yet our public servants and presses, even our entertainment programs, all lie in some fashion every day as part of their accepted function. As Christians we are at war with theft and swindling, yet, if we work in any of the government's social services, we see the taxpayer swindled to subsidize incompetence, laziness, and extravagance. As Christians we are at war with vice and sensuality, yet the cities in which we live actually glamorize lawless sexuality in a hundred ways.

If we turn to the more intimate sphere of personal and family life, the rift between the ethos of the world and the ethos of the Church is just as wide. Few of us do not have somewhere among our friends somebody who has been divorced and has taken another spouse. Now the world is bringing the family a new menace—artificial insemination. If anything can reveal the gaping chasm between the ethos of the Church and the ethos of the world, it is surely that. Observe, please, that it is not the world's outcasts, the world's criminals, who are practicing this outrage upon the human personality, this fraud upon the next generation; it is, rather, the respectable men and women with status in society and in the community. Yet, to us Christians, they are, in their deeds, more grossly at fault morally than the prostitute at the street corner or the embezzler doing his ten years in the penitentiary. Make no mistake about it! Artificial insemination measures the distance between the morality of the world and the morality of the Church. Other things being equal, the respectable physician, with his syringe and his test tube, with his air-conditioned Cadillac and his 'ivy-league" suit, is, in the Church's eyes, a far bigger sinner than the cheap prostitute or the debt-ridden manager who has juggled his firm's accounts. Neither the prostitute nor the embezzler is pretending to be God; they have been led astray, in the first place, by the snares of the flesh; but the physician is guilty of the very sin for which Lucifer was condemned to hell: he is trying to be God Almighty; in matching men with women, eye with eye, and brain with brain, to fashion a future generation of his own devising, he is trying to play God.

Any informed Christian who has heard or read the utterances of physicians who practice and encourage this violation of manhood, womanhood, and childhood will have been struck by two things. First, the total disregard for the interests of the children who are being produced by artificial insemination; no consideration at all is given to their welfare; all arguments in favour of the practice are based upon consideration for the selfish satisfactions of the mother and the pretender who will be called "father." Any practice in relation to the family which is based upon principles disregarding the children's interests is *ipso facto* unjustified. The family exists to protect and nurture the children, not to provide fun for the parents. The second thing is this: the Christian is horrified by the arrogance and presumption of medical men who are taking upon themselves the right to decide upon tangled matters which involve legal, moral, and spiritual problems of the deepest sort. Such men are attempting to construct the next generation to the pattern of their own text book blueprints, without hesitating to question their right to do so.

The issue is a basic one, and an important one—not the least because it is still in its infancy. The practice of artificial insemination could destroy the last remnants of Christian culture. It has been the opinion of many wise and far-seeing men, since

115

even before the days of Aldous Huxley's *Brave New World*, that in the long run physicists, for all their capacity to annihilate human civilization and even human life, are never likely to constitute so dire a threat to truly human interests as the biologists with their desire to produce human life under conditions which by-pass the family system. For the next ten years it will be necessary, utterly so, for humane thinkers and moralists who guard our culture not to fasten their attention so exclusively to the menace of hydrogen bombs and ballistic missiles that they fail to notice behind their backs what the medical men are up to. We could find ourselves, in twenty years or so, with international peace reasonably assured, atomic power happily harnessed in the interest of civilization, and a million boys and girls in their teens with impostors standing where their fathers should have stood; a million boys and girls perhaps despising their mothers and hating their stepfathers. A generation, in which girls could mate with their own fathers and brothers in utter ignorance, must now be taken seriously as a possible donation to society by modern genetics.

Urgent as this matter is, it is our purpose to pursue it further: we want only to illustrate how the ethos of the world and the ethos of the Church are in conflict, and the practice and defence of artificial insemination is evidence enough. Like the practice and defence of divorce, it is symptomatic of the world's hedonistic values and the world's worship of appetites and emotions. You will make no progress in the world except by adapting yourself to the world, by accepting the standards of the world. You will make no progress if you attack the world. Let us put it succinctly. Divorce and remarriage will no longer prevent you from rising to the top of your profession; it will not keep you from becoming a United States Senator or a State Governor, but an outspoken attack upon divorce may well wipe away any chances of promotion at the office or wherever it is that you work. It is as simple as that. Fit in with the world, and it will treat you well; speak out against the world, and it will treat you ill, you will lose your "friends"—they will fall away from you like leaves in the autumn, and you will be thought odd, difficult, bigoted, narrow-minded.

It costs something to be in the world and yet not of it. It cost God—in the person of His Son and the fact of the Crucifixion, and we have no reason whatsoever to think that it will not cost us. In the paragraph above we saw the costliness of the divine-human blend; we see it firsthand in our own relation to the world and in our most personal desires. Just as our worldly ambition—the search for recognition, respect, promotion, reward—may have to be crucified if we are to live faithfully in the Church, so our private desires may have to be crucified too. There is no good thing that costs nothing. As our early communion may cost an hour's sleep, so a visit to the sick or lonely may cost an evening at home or an after-dinner snooze on the sofa. As our changing a tire for a stranded motorist will put grease on our hands, so our acceptance of an aging relative into our home destroys the long-enjoyed dwaddling in the bathroom. We cannot purchase good for ourselves or others without paying a price. It just can't be done. A happy marriage is sustained by the sacrifice of thousands of little things. Our union with our Lord in His Church is something like that: each single stone in the fabric of its stability is made of hundreds of self-denials.

We are invited to serve the world by serving ourselves, but the double loyalty—to the world and to ourselves—must be repudiated if we are to live in obedience to God. It is not always that way, but many times a day service to God involves treachery to the world and betrayal of the world's cult of material prosperity. More often service to

God demands denial of self. That is not always true, of course: music may be a great delight for a church organist, and bedside chatting may be natural to a parish caller; but in any case, God's service always puts a rein upon man's natural desires and a break upon his self-assertiveness. The tension produced by blending life in the Church with life in the world is totally eased only by death.

It may not be amiss to say that the modern conception of man's earthly life, as popularly cherished in the civilized west, is peculiarly hostile to truly Christian thinking. The Christian is taught to see this life on earth as subordinate to life in other realms of creation. He sees this life as *less stable, less permanent*—something less than eternal life with God in heaven. In other words, the Christian is merely *on the way*: his life is passed *en route*. That is the kind of life it is—a pilgrimage, a progress through time and space, past death to what lies beyond. What the Christian thinks about the next life determines his thinking about this life, and that is what distinguishes him from the unbeliever.

The unbeliever treats this life as *the* thing—the sum and substance of everything; insofar as there is stability, regularity, and permanence, and a ground under our feet and a shelter over his head, this is it. Afterwards, well—who knows? Darkness, annihilation, some vague twilight existence endured vaporously between limitless space and the medium's table? For the unbeliever life outside this earth is uncertain; for the Christian that life is assured. For the unbeliever this world is a place to settle down in, but for the Christian it is a place to be passed through—enjoyed, yes, but nothing to be chained to. That surely is the greatest distinction of all. The modern mind regards early life as something to take root in: it is the ground and basis of all value, all meaning, all joy. Earthly life is *trusted* by unbelievers to the degree that Christians trust the next one. For the unbeliever, this life is the only thing there is to trust.

Contemporary thought and action, in the political and social sphere, and equally in the private and personal sphere, takes much of its impulse from a fundamental *rootedness* in earthly life. Unless we reckon this rootedness as a potent factor in the contemporary mental environment, we shall fail to see the nature and the seriousness of the gap which divides us from our unbeliever acquaintances. A more important reason for knowing how a pagan trusts in the finality and stability of earthly life is that we Christians need to be constantly on guard in order to prevent ourselves from falling

into the same error. It is fatally easy, in these days
of materialistic propaganda handed out on all sides,
in these days of mass welfare services which hedge
us about with securities from the cradle to the
grave—it is fatally easy for Christians to be
infected with a confidence in earthly life which
does not require to be justified or judged by refer-
ence to anything surer or higher. Above all, we
must be watchful against the pernicious temptation to pervert our holy religion into one more
welfare service—one more instrument for bringing social solace and personal stimulus to the fundamentally earthbound soul. It is blasphemy to
treat the Christian faith as one more national
benefit—something designed to lighten the load
and cheer the path of men rooted and grounded
in time and place.

The only safeguard against this damning sac-
rilege is the purity of the Church herself—a purity
that involves our own faithfulness. We can never
hope to be truly faithful unless we daily remind
ourselves that this earth is not our true home, that
here is no abiding city. By our baptism we are
born into a kingdom other than the world's, by it
we are rooted in a soil other than the earth's: yet
neither citizenship in that kingdom nor growth in
its soil is incompatible with a joyful passage

through this time and this place, but each is certainly incompatible with settling down here as though this earth were one's true and only home.

The Church's attitude towards the modern world is made all the more difficult to appreciate because so many people today who claim to be Christians have no understanding of the great doctrines to which, by their baptism, they are committed. This, as all informed Christians know, has desperate consequences. Indeed, nothing is sadder in our present situation, and nothing more fraught with tragic tensions, than the fact that the pseudo-Christian humanism, so prevalent in our midst and so cleverly masquerading as an ally of the Catholic Faith, is often fundamentally ranged against it. Let us consider a single antithesis.

Pseudo-Christian humanism presupposes an absent God. The Catholic Faith offers us a present God. The difference between recognition of an absent God and recognition of a present God is perhaps deeper than the difference between recognition of an absent God and the total denial of God's existence. Consider the point seriously, for it is a grave one, and the proper understanding of it can keep us from being self-deceived. Pseudo-Christian humanism, which appears to be the religion of many of our contemporaries, offers us an absent God—a God so far away from His creation that men have to spend their lives trying to make sure that He even exists. So remote is He from this world that men search laboriously and intensely for clues, however slight, which might provide at least circumstantial evidence that somewhere, somehow, God truly lives. That is the God of the pseudo-Christian humanists, among whom many of us pass our working lives and at whose sides perhaps we sometimes worship. God is so withdrawn, so concealed, even so disguised that any man's guess about Him is as good as another's. He is a God of whom man's knowledge is *bound* to be merely conjectural, tentative, subjective, and individual. He is a God about whom each of us has the right to have his privately established and often unchangeable opinions and feelings.

That is the God of the pseudo-Christian humanists. The ones who learn most about Him are the intellectuals who happen to have the brains and the leisure to spend a lifetime in search of Him. They investigate the religions of history, they explore the works of the great philosophers, they weigh the testimony of holy men and mystics of a dozen creeds, they sample the findings of scholars in a score of different fields of research—from anthropology to paranormal psychology; having worn out their eyes and their years in study, they eventually arrive at the realization that a Supreme Spiritual Being resides at the back of the universe. They have found their way to God, and they write books to urge others to follow painstakingly their own rewarding path.

It would be wrong to ridicule any man's spiritual pilgrimage; but in the name of truth itself there is a duty to attack the current notion that God is so cut off from our world that only through a course of arduous and advanced study can men attain to a glimpse of His reality. Then too it must be pointed out that a god who thus hides himself from the eyes of all but the brainiest is not the God of the Gospel, not the God of the Church, not the God of history. A god who makes himself known only to the "egg-heads," or to people who have the ability and will to study learned books, has little in common with the God of the Catholic Faith.

Why must we press this distinction? Because all sorts of heretical notions and attitudes, all sorts of half-Christian half-truths have sprouted and flourished under the shelter of the Absent-God myth of the pseudo-Christian. Many of the misconceptions which we have to counter daily, and which even seep into the Church and disturb the faithful, are ultimately derived from this myth. For instance, we are continually having to deal with people who are suspicious of dogma and openly claim that religious doctrines are all "a matter of opinion." It is possible, of course, to hold that religious doctrines are all "a matter of opinion," but only if the absent, unrevealed god is presupposed. It is possible to hold that one man's individual view in a theological matter is as valid as the next man's view, but only if an absent, unrevealed god is presupposed. If God is here, now, before us—present, active, revealed, encountered, and known, all talk of conflicting individual "opinions" about Him and His ways is nothing more than a "blast of vain doctrine." Such talk presupposes that God has abandoned the world and left it in darkness. Such talk presupposes an untruth. If God has indeed shown His hand plainly within creation, if He has manifested Himself and continues to manifest Himself within our temporal universe, there can be no cause for men to grope in darkness for some evidence of His existence, no cause for men to conduct private researches into the matter of His nature. If God has shown His hand clearly and openly, if He is here and now among us, we men have about us authentic testimony to His existence, His nature, and His purpose for us.

The Catholic Faith teaches that God has inserted Himself in our world. In three ways our Lord has dwelt and dwells here among us in this time and place: in His Incarnate Body, in His Mystical Body, and in His Sacramental Body. This three-fold indwelling of the divine in the temporal is the expression and the guarantee of God's love for men. If the indwelling of the Divine Body is not fact, Catholic Faith is in error. If it is fact, as we believe it is, all beliefs which presuppose an absent God are themselves in error. It is as simple as that. Even though the "beliefs" in question are expressed in a Christian vocabulary, and even though that expression is clothed in many technical terms, if it is presupposed that God is absent from His world, those "beliefs" themselves are in error.

The presupposition that God is absent may be expressed in a view which on the surface appears to be harmless enough to the uninstructed, and such is the view that theological convictions are a matter of individual opinion and not a matter of objective truth and binding authority. Let us not mince words, either out of dangerous tenderness to ourselves or out of mistaken indulgence to others. If God has inserted himself into the sphere of the temporal and the human, at the point where that insertion cuts into time and space you have truth and authority, absolute and unconditional. Such, we believe, is the truth of the Catholic Faith and the authority of the Church; but the whole temper of modern civilization is alien to the notion of absolute truth and unconditional authority in the religious sphere. Right there, then, you have a sharp and deep cleavage between the Church and the world. Over this issue the Church and the world give each other the lie. Moreover, all those who are within the Church and yet claim that religious conviction is a matter of individual opinion, and all who are within the Church and yet contest the idea of objective doctrinal truth or resist the idea of the Church's authority, are, in this respect, willy-nilly allies of the world.

That's the way it is, logically and necessarily. Some of us might well wish that it did not follow so logically and so necessarily, but it does.

Almighty God, then, has inserted Himself within the framework of the natural order which He Himself made. At His touch a woman brought the Divine Incarnate Body to birth. At His touch the Church our Mother brings the Divine Sacramental Body to birth. Reflect, please, upon the touch of God and what it accomplishes. Does not God impinge upon our world in a richly godlike fashion? Has not His touch a recognizable stamp —one characteristic of the Creator who devised and constructed our universe? Has not His touch the mark of the Maker of stars and streams and growing things, of flowers and men and beasts? Certainly it is a restorative and transfiguring touch —a touch at which life awakens and stirs. It is a touch which everywhere achieves miracles of creativity and transformation. From a human womb, the Incarnate Body; from children of the womb, the Mystical Body; from an earthly grave, the Resurrected Body; from the fruits of the earth, the Sacramental Body. In all the ways God would *be* with us, and each is indeed an Emmanuel, "which being interpreted is, God with us." How determined God is not to abandon us to our world!

The insertion of the Body of God into human history has a corollary (a corollary for which the present writer is indebted to Peguy): the unceasing insertion of human history into the Body of God. Human history—the history which, among other things, is made by you and me in our daily acts of obedience and our daily sins—is inserted into the Body of God. That is what we are about, you and I, today, now, this very moment. We are inserting human history into the Body of God. We are building up the Body of Christ; either that or else we are wounding and damaging the Body of Christ.

Peguy, speaking through the mouth of Clio, the Muse of history, has expressed this illuminating idea with characteristic charm and vividness.

The least of sinners, the least of sins, wounds Jesus eternally. There you have Christianity. And I, history, throughout my long history, can do nothing which does not interest Jesus, God, naturally and as though physically. I cannot commit anything temporarally which is not inserted, physically as it were, into the body of God himself. There, my child, is Christianity for you. Real. The rest, my friend, all the rest—come my dear Alphandry, come now, let us say the rest is good enough for the comparative history of religions. It is the binding, the eternal, temporal binding, the link, the inlay of the one in the other, that incrucification as it were, which makes Christianity. The rest is good material for schoolmasters.*

That is what we Christians are about. We are

*Charles Peguy, *Temporal and Eternal*, trans. Alexander Dru (New York: Harper & Brothers).

building up the Body of Christ, or else we are tear-
ing down the Body of Christ. The world is about
its own work, and that is a very different thing.
We are about God's work—or we *should* be. The
servants of the world (are we perhaps after all
secretly among them?) take their stand in the
world; the servants of the world (can we confi-
dently exclude ourselves from their number?) root
and ground themselves in time; but as Christians
we take our stand at that point of intersection
where eternity cuts into time, where God plunges
into history. As Churchmen we claim membership
of that Body by which God inserts Himself into
our temporal world. The unbelievers take a different stand—not in a world broken open to heaven
and to hell, but in a complete, slef-contained world,
a world in which there is neither God nor devil to
reckon with, a rounded, unopened universe that
goes rolling down from nothingness to nothingness,
unwatched, untended, and untouched.

We who are Christians inhabit a world exposed
to God, and we cannot escape the divine watchfulness, the divine tending. By the grace of the Holy
Spirit we have been brought within reach of the
divine touch—the touch which once put a Christ
in the stable, held in the arms of Mary, the touch
which today puts a Christ on the altar, held in

the arms of Holy Church, the touch which made saints of a skeptical Thomas and faltering Peter, and the touch which can make a Church from material like you and me.

Thus, once again we arrive at the conclusion that if we who call ourselves Christians treat our world, for practical purposes, as a closed system, shut off from the infinite, we miss the whole point of the faith we profess. The Church provides powerful safeguards against this error. The Catholic Doctrine of the Incarnation, the Catholic Doctrine of the Church, and the Catholic Doctrine of the Eucharist—all have this in common: they testify to the doctrines of the exposed world and the inserted God. If, however, we think and speak and behave as though contact with God were possible only through some vague system of spiritual telegraphy which reaches out from a locked-up temporal universe to a remote and nebulous infinity, we virtually deny the Doctrine of the Inserted God. Again, if we focus our mental microscopes on the printed word of the scholars (even the biblical scholars), or direct our mental telescopes at the metaphysical first cause and metaphysical absolutes, thinking that only by minute and abstruse study can we glimpse a trace of the divine reality, then we too virtually deny the Doctrine of the Inserted God—the God who is always about us in His Mystical Body and in His Sacramental Body.

It is so easy in the modern world to allow our "Christianity" to degenerate into a cherished fantasy from which God is virtually banished. It is so easy to turn our backs upon God-in-the-world, to turn against that uncomfortably close and challenging God-in-the Church, and then manufacture an altogether remoter and less demanding god for our private use and consolation—to set up a god who can be assembled like a jigsaw puzzle with bits picked up in anthologies of *Spiritual Insights from All Creeds* and *Selections from the Pantheistic Poets*. It is easy. It is also absurd. It is absurd to seek toilsomely in our world for divine footprints left here long ago in some hurried passage through temporality, some casual and half-forgotten divine encounter with the earth. Our world has been subjected to a *full-scale* divine intrusion; and it is divinely entered and inhabited every day. It is absurd to seek for the faint, barely decipherable footprints of God when He stands right at our side—and there is His face to look at. It is absurd to try to call up once every month on an unreliable spiritual telephone a God who in fact sits always in His house and ours, and asks us to eat at His table. To act thus is to blind ourselves to what is about us and to what we ourselves are. The Church is about us, and we are the Church: God is in us, and we are in Him.

It is no doubt true that in certain respects relations between the Church and the world are more awkward now than they have been for many centuries—more awkward because in some quarters communication between believers and unbelievers has broken down. Churchmen need not blame themselves alone for this, yet the difficulty must not be glossed over. While it is possible that a frank admission that Christians and secularists no longer talk the same language may clear the air of much confusion, the awkwardness remains. It can be exemplified by comparing the situation today with that of the last century. One of the great debates between believers and unbelievers last century centered around the question, "Is the Old Testament literally true?" Believers foolishly said "Yes." Unbelievers exultantly said "No."

When we compare the debate with some of the twentieth-century intellectual conflicts between Christians and non-Christians, we can scarcely prevent ourselves from being a little envious of our grandparents. How comparatively slight, how comparatively narrow, we murmur, was the gap between the believer and the unbeliever last century! Slight and narrow indeed, for they were both *answering the same question*. Think of it: to the twentieth-century mind, aware of the recent struggle between Christian philosophers and positivists, it suggests a meeting of ideas so notable as almost to indicate agreement. Both parties recognized the same question as meaningful and important. Each party recognized the other party as having given a meaningful and important, though false, reply. For both parties the question conveyed the same meaning; for both of them the two answers carried the same connotation.

The divergence between the Church and the philosophical world is now so wide in some quarters that there are no longer any common questions —questions recognized by each party. No longer does the Christian say, "I believe in God," and the unbeliever reply, "I see what you mean, but I myself don't believe in God." On the contrary, the contemporary unbeliever (if he is a positivist) replies, "Don't talk nonsense. No meaning can be attached to those three letters, G, O, D, unless you print them in a different order. As they stand, they do not constitute a valid symbol of anything known. GOD does not stand for something we have experienced, like BUCKET or COW. It is a noise in the mouth, like GLIP or NURGE—nothing more."

Again, let us be honest about all this. The positivist thinks and says that we Christians are talking nonsense. We Christians *know* that the positivist is the one who is talking nonsense. We Christians *know* therefore that many of the men holding important academic posts are talking nonsense. We *know* that, but where do we go from here?

One thing ought to be clear. We don't go into debate as though we were going to have a polite discussion with nineteenth-century rationalists—there aren't many nineteenth-century rationalists left, and we can't debate with a person who says that our words don't mean anything. If our words mean nothing to him, how can his words mean anything to us? If we give meaning to the very words by which he attempts to discredit or deny the meaning of the Christian vocabulary, we are betraying truth. Because the words in the Christian vocabulary do have meaning, questions can indeed come into the arena of debate between Christians and unbelievers. For example, there is the question, "Is there a God?" There are also questions which *cannot* be debated because to allow the question ("Has the word GOD a meaning?")

135

would declare nonsense to be sense. The point is that in some quarters the debatable questions are no longer at issue: only the undebatable ones are raised.

Perhaps we should be content to leave the undebatable ones alone; you cannot play a game with a person who breaks all the rules. You cannot argue Christianity with a positivist.* We don't have to worry about this, nor should we be over-awed by the strength of skepticism† in the philosophy departments of our colleges and universities.

We must not pursue too far the topic of "philosophical" opposition to the Faith. We have used it here as only an example, like that of artificial insemination, to illustrate the rift between the Church and the world, this time in the intellecual sphere. There are plenty of other examples. For instance, in the matter of divorce and remarriage there is no question common to the world and the Church. The world says that there is such a question as "Is marriage indissoluble?" But we Christians can't allow that to be a debatable ques-

---

*A positivist is one who says that you can't argue about something unless you *know* that something. You can argue about the paper these words are printed on because you see and feel the paper, but you can't argue about the thoughts conveyed by the words.——ED.

†A skeptic is one who says that all knowledge is uncertain——that you can't even be sure about the paper. This book that you are holding may not be book at all, but something else!——ED.

tion at all. By its very nature, marriage *is* indissoluble. That's what marriage is—an *indissoluble union*. The "question" about it is like the "question" about soap, "Can soap clean the hands?" That is exactly what soap is—something that cleans the hands. If it can't clean, it isn't soap. If the union is not indissoluble, it is not a marriage.

We must not think ourselves thrown into the midst of a lively debate in today's world, for there is no debate. The only debate that ever took place broke up in disorder some years ago. Now there is nothing but chaos of error and self-deception on one hand, and on the other hand truth, which is our Lord. We must affirm that truth. We must reveal not only our conviction of the truth but also our willingness to defend that truth. It has to be affirmed verbally, but more especially it has to be affirmed in our lives—in prayer, in obedience, in worship, in witness. I repeat, *affirmation is the need of the hour*.

We do not need more debates, more discussions: it is foolish to try to carry on a debate when there is no motion, no chairman, and when the platform has collapsed and people in the audience have turned to fighting among themselves. Leave all that alone and go out and do something. There are people who want to hear the truth, some of them are eager to hear it, and they are not going to be satisfied with debates and discussions; it is the business of the Church, your business and mine, to see that the truth is told, that it is presented, that it is affirmed.

A firm and unyielding presentation of the truth is the need of our time, and that is exactly what is demanded of the Church. It is sad that we must admit it, but the Church misses almost every one of its present-day opportunities. As though in a dream, the Church gloriously persists in fighting an enemy who was defeated thirty years ago. If the Church has a besetting weakness, it is this: it insists on tackling foes who have already been beaten; it attempts to deal with problems that have already been solved; it readies itself to overcome tomorrow obstacles that were removed during the night. In intellectual matters, the dominant devil of yesterday was rationalism,* and that was something that could be argued with; but the dominant devil today is positivism, and that is something nobody can argue with. Nevertheless the Church goes on debating with imaginary rationalists. In moral matters, the dominant devil

*Rationalism is the theory that reason is a source of knowledge in itself, and that it is superior to and independent of what we feel, or see, or taste, or hear. The rationalist says that the supernatural can be explained by reason.—Ed.

138

of yesterday was cruelty, and it was necessary to preach tolerance and charity; but the dominant devil today is lawlessness, and it is necessary to preach obedience and self-surrender, to press the claims of authority and discipline. Nevertheless the Church goes on preaching toleration to souls dying of laxity, preaching charity to hearts poisoned by easy-going indulgence of anything and everything, and, it would seem, preaching indifference to a world made different by the Incarnation.

We need affirmation, not debate; we need discipline, not open-mindedness; we need obedience, not expansiveness. Last century it was the great social reformers and humanitarians who met the crying need of their day. Now, by contract, it is the monks and nuns who, withdrawn and disciplined, meet the need of our day. They, the "religious" as they are called, are in the vanguard of the struggle against lawlessness, against the arrogant disregard of man's creaturely status which is now trying to construct a time-locked materialistic Utopia—a virtual hell on earth. We who flatter ourselves that we are playing a part in things, that we are helping the great Christian cause in a practical on-the-spot fashion, have need to remind ourselves that the most practical, the most potent reply to the lawless and man-centered materialism of today is the reply of the religious. How else can disobedience be countered except by obedience, or sensuality except by chastity, or worldliness except by poverty?

Yet how often do our bishops and priests encourage us to consider the religious life? How often do we hear sermons on obedience, on chastity, on poverty? How often is our search for truth, and the practice of it, diverted into the blind alleys of programs, committees, and campaigns, and meetings? In a world already too busy with itself, the Church would load us with even more busy-ness.

Every age has its own errors, and each demands different treatment. Although the Church's fundamental message and mission are unchangeable throughout the centuries, the emphasis in her practice and teaching is shifted according to the needs of the moment, and each shift is calculated to counter the effect of a temporary aberration. Furthermore, the Holy Spirit Himself operates to affect such shifts of emphasis.

So it is that what is needed to meet the spiritual, intellectual, and moral aberrations of our day is obviously an emphasis on precisely those aspects of Christian faith and practice which you and I are concerned to press. Our age is loose in its thinking and insanely averse to intellectual clarity and certitude, and so it is therefore especially urgent to press the firm dogmatic affirmations of Catholic doctrine. Our age is lax in its allegiances and sentimental in its social codes, and it is therefore specially urgent for us to press the Catholic conception of the Church, to emphasize the authority of its traditions and its hierarchy, and the strict obligations of membership. Our age is evasive in the matter of formal observances and nebulous in its spirituality, and so we must therefore stress the power of the ordered sacramental system to nourish and discipline the life of the soul, to sanctify the whole man with its blend of worship and concrete embodiment. Above all else, our age is given over to vain confidence in earthly achievement and earthly pleasure, and so it is therefore our inescapable duty to press upon our contemporaries the essential other worldiness of the Christian message, and to highlight the Church as the Supernatural Body of men and women living in the life of the Risen Christ. We can sum up the appropriate Christian emphasis in our day as one which would press doctrinal *certainty*, ecclesiastical *authority*, and supernatural *orientation*. These three: the dogmatic, the institutional and sacramental, and the spiritual—the Truth, the Way, and the Life.

Somebody will ask, "To what end?" That is
a question which is often in our minds as we consider the rigours of Christian discipline and the
Church's way. The end, we say, is the glory of
God: the love and service of God, for which we
were created. But that does not quite answer
another question—one which sometimes hangs
around in the back of the mind. It is a question
with a "curve"; it is such a shaming question that
we are reluctant to bring it out into the open and
face up to it. Perhaps, in origin, it is the Devil's
own question—probably he put it in our minds.
Certainly it has the Devil's favor. "Why bother?"
the question goes, "God's love and mercy are
boundless. He is not going to be defeated in the
end. If He has created men and women for glory,
He will see that they attain that glory. What sense,
if any, is to be found in the Crucifixion and the
Resurrection unless salvation has been won for *all*
men? Salvation for all: that is surely the only
logical and loving conclusion to the vast experiment of man-making. Are we not bothering over-
much to make the Christian life an arduous thing?"

The theory of universal salvation has such
appealing attractions that we are compelled to
remind ourselves from time to time of its peculiar
difficulties. On the surface it seems to fit so well

with the world's notion of a loving God that we want to forget it clashes with reason's concept of a purposeful God. It is perhaps safer for men to say, "We don't fully comprehend the nature of God's love," than to say, "In the end, God makes nonsense of free will and minimizes the distinction between good and evil." This is one of the many issues in Christian teaching about which we should think concretely rather than abstractly. Phrases like "universal salvation" and "God's boundless love and mercy" are dangerously abstract. They sound good and roll off the tongue well, but while uttering them or hearing them we can lose sight of the real living subject of salvation, the free individual man or woman.

Consider the individual. He must die. His earthly life will end and he will take leave of this finite scene. If there is any truth at all in Christian teaching, the individual sooner or later will meet the God who made him and all that he has known. Is it going to matter, then, whether he, the individual, has lived increasingly in the Holy Spirit, faithfully in membership of the Church, arduously in the discipline of the Christian way? Is it going to matter whether he has lived thus, or has lived in increasing worldliness, covetousness, sensuality, and self-centeredness—deaf to every one of God's words? Is it going to matter? Or is freedom to be laughed off, at last, by a benign God as a subtle joke at man's expense? Examine the idea carefully, for that is what "universal salvation" appears to mean—that somehow, sometime, God will have to admit that Christians have taken the conflict between good and evil a little too seriously. Are we prepared to accept such a notion of divine judgment—accept a denouncement which reveals the greatest saints to have been victims of a trick? Will the hosts of heaven laugh at men for having been taken in? We made them *think* it mattered— this deceptive difference between good and evil!"

Such a notion is one from which very sound Christian impulse and every healthy Christian intelligence shrinks in abhorrence. In other words, the theory that we call "universal salvation" turns out, when we picture it concretely, to be blasphemous and obscene. Let us hope we are wrong, but let us not deny that our understanding in the finite world will allow us to see no other alternative. Salvation and damnation are both real, or else moral freedom is, in the end, nothing but a mockery.

If salvation and damnation are alike real, where does God's mercy fit in? The answer is, of course, that it leaves man free to the very end. Turn again from abstractions and picture man's lot concretely. An individual dies. If he is in the way of salvation, he eventually comes face to face with God. However great his sins, however deep his shame, however bitter his tears of self-condemnation, there can be no doubt that the vision of God will evoke from him the glad recognition, "This is what I was seeking. This is what the best part of me was always trying to serve, to reach, to praise. This is what I glimpsed in my least selfish, least confined moments. This is what, deeply and inwardly, I have always known myself meant for. In this Person is every truth, every value, every virtue that I have ever tasted, recognized, or dreamed of. This is heaven."

But what if the individual is *not* in the way of salvation? What if he has worshipped earth and sense and self up to the very end? Surely, if we may suppose a vision of God for him, he must, at the first moment of meeting, recognize what he has opposed. "That," he must say, "is what I have always been up against. My whole life I have fought against it. There it is. It has wanted to claim and consume me. It has sought to destroy my attachment to my own identity. It has tried to corrode the center of all my pleasures, my wishes, my desires. It was and is eternally my foe.

It has tried to trap and ensnare me. All my life I have sought to evade its cunning contrivances to come between me and myself. Now I see it plainly for what it is: the utterly and objectively Other, the bitterest and surest foe of my struggling self; the offensive and encroaching Other, which my soul abhors." That is damnation.